Church Life
Building on the Foundation of Jesus Christ

Clay Sterrett

Extra copies and/or a catalog of other materials may be obtained from:
CFC Literature
P.O. Box 245
Staunton, VA 24402-0245
ISBN 0-9760454-0-0
Printed by Old Paths Tract Society, Inc., Shoals, IN

Introduction:
On What Foundation
Are We Building?

DeVern Fromke, a dear friend and one of my favorite
spiritual authors, granted me permission to share this very
personal and painful story.

Many years ago when I was a young man in the
ministry, God sent a gracious awakening into the area
where I lived. After graduating from a college on the
West Coast, I went back to Missouri. Here, the Holy
Spirit began to work in many of the churches. . . . By
His wonderful grace, hundreds were truly converted,
and many church members were revived. Eventually,
we prayed and became burdened to establish a training
center, a "Boot Camp," for youth. On eighty acres, we
built thirteen buildings. We had lots of enthusiasm and
invaluable help from the builders.

Then suddenly, something strange happened. I was
away when my mother sent me a telegram. Someone
had slipped in overnight – while everyone was absent
and the property was vacant – and set all the buildings
on fire. I read the telegram in disbelief and cried out,
"God, we were doing this for You!" I'm ashamed to

admit it, but my heart began to complain, "God why didn't You take care of Your property?!"[1]

It was during this great trial of faith that Fromke began to understand a lesson that would radically affect the rest of his life and ministry: the importance of building on the right foundation. The Holy Spirit caused this Scripture to come alive to him.

By the grace God has given me, I laid a foundation as an expert builder, and someone else is building on it. But each one should be careful how he builds. For no one can lay any foundation other than the one already laid, which is Jesus Christ. If any man builds on this foundation using gold, silver, costly stones, wood, hay or straw, his work will be shown for what it is, because the Day will bring it to light. It will be revealed with fire, and the fire will test the quality of each man's work. If what he has built survives, he will receive his reward. If it is burned up, he will suffer loss; he himself will be saved, but only as one escaping through the flames.[2]

After his horrible loss, Fromke said he was not angry with God, but just simply asked a question, "Why, Lord?" The Lord answered him in a way he did not expect.

Then I saw myself standing in a long line. I do not say it was a dream or vision, but suddenly I became conscious of the Judgment Seat or the "Bema" of God, with Jesus seated on His Judgment Throne. I stood in line with many of my friends. Some of them approached the Lord with their arms filled with wood, hay, and stubble. Suddenly, the moment that His piercing eyes of fire from the Throne hit their wood, hay, and stubble, it burned, leaving behind only traces of ashes. They were saved, but had nothing to show for a lifetime of work. One by one, I saw different ones coming under His piercing eyes of fire.

Then, it was my turn. I looked at my arms. I had done much in my work for the Lord. I hoped that there might have been a little gold. Just as I stepped forward, the Lord pulled the curtain shut. "Not yet," He said. How relieved and pleased was I to hear His words, "Not yet." It is as real to me now as though it were yesterday. I thought I heard Him say, "There's still time to get gold, silver, and precious stone-that which is wrought by the Holy Spirit's transforming work in your life."[3]

Through this costly, sobering experience, Fromke began to understand the difference between a life work that is built upon THE FOUNDATION and one which is merely built on "another foundation." It was not just doing "works for Him," *but Him.* It was not just "building for Christ," but it was building the very *life of Christ* into others.[4] Fromke had begun to realize the necessity of *building on the foundation of Jesus Christ.*

Will Our Works Stand the Test of Fire?

How about our works? Would they stand the test of the Lord's fire? It is a scary thought that we could be very successful according to the world's standards, yet when it comes to the Judgment Seat of Christ, all of our works will be burned up. The Lord, who sees the hidden things, will detect any wrong motives and improper foundations in our lives.

Therefore, let us consider two different ways of building.

WHAT IS THE DIFFERENCE?

- A great ministry by human standards. (**Wood, hay, straw** come in large quantities.)

- A spiritual work which pleases the Heavenly Father. (*Gold, silver, costly stones* rare.)

- Centered in a man. (e.g., "Our wonderful pastor"; "God's anointed prophet")

- Centered in Christ. (Jesus the Head of the body; Our Exalted One; our All in all)

- Much energy spent and much busy activity.

- Waiting on God for the ministry of the Holy Spirit.

- Emphasis on programs which work. ("What will keep the people happy?")

- Emphasis on the will of God. ("Lord, what are you doing that we can join you in?")

ANOTHER FOUNDATION	THE FOUNDATION
- Building my own kingdom.	- Building God's kingdom.
- Ambitious for my reputation	- Desiring God's glory.
- Making a name for myself.	- Lifting up Jesus' name.

(WHAT ARE THE HIDDEN MOTIVES?)

For no one can lay any foundation other than the one already laid, which is Jesus Christ . . .

Because we do not know the depths of depravity still lurking in our own hearts, we must ask God to search our hearts. He alone sees the hidden motives. *Man looks at the outward appearance, but the Lord looks at the heart.*[5] *He will bring to light what is hidden in darkness and will expose the motives of men's hearts.*[6]

Is our work usually done in the energy of the flesh or in the power of the Spirit? Are we doing what we do to earn the accolades of man or to make ourselves feel good, or do we work for the glory of God? In our church, who is ultimately getting all the attention – a man or Jesus Christ?

The New Testament Church – A Model to Follow

It is the purpose of this book to examine various facets of church life in light of the New Testament pattern and to encourage us to build rightly upon the foundation of Jesus Christ. It is this author's view that the church portrayed in the New Testament is more than an interesting history lesson; it is a model to follow. Dr. Charles Farah encouraged this view:

> It is my understanding that the book of Acts was written not primarily to give us history of the primitive church, but to furnish us with pattern insights into the nuts and bolts of what the Church not only was, but was meant to be . . . . *As the epistles are normative for teaching, so the book of Acts is normative for the life and experience of the church.*[7]

This may be a radical idea for some believers. Do we really agree with his statement, *the book of Acts is normative for the life and experience of the church?* If so, how far removed are we from the New Testament model? Do we look to the book of Acts and the rest of the New Testament as a pattern to follow?

When we say we are pursuing the "New Testament" model or pattern, that does not mean we are looking for the exact same characteristics in every church. God is not in the cloning business; all churches (and all Christians) do not have to look the same. There can be distinct emphases, different structures and forms of government, and various methods of ministry and outreach. The New Testament churches were not like peas in a pod. There is no detailed, universal blueprint for every local congregation. Our great God delights in variety and so should we.

Our Own Experience – Still Pursuing the Pattern

For over thirty-five years our own local congregation in Virginia has tried to pursue the New Testament pattern in the way we pursue church life. Many of the concepts presented in this book, such as leadership by plural leaders and working with other congregations, are not just theological concepts; they have become reality to us. We have seen some good fruit from this pursuit of the New Testament ideal. However, we also feel we are learners on a lifetime journey. If one was to visit us, he would quickly become aware of some of our deficiencies. No matter what amount of success any church obtains or how closely they might attain to their image of New Testament church, they must walk humbly and embrace brethren in Christ who may have different approaches to church life. We will find in the body of Christ many dear saints who use certain methods different from us, who call themselves by titles we would never use, or who seem to take a different approach in attracting new members. All of these matters are secondary and on such issues, *each one should be fully convinced in his own mind.*[8]

This book is dedicated to all brethren who desire to see the church built on the foundation of Jesus Christ, and for those who yearn to see something that is more a work of the Holy Spirit than the work of mere men or clever organization. For all who love the Lord Jesus, we want to reassure you: the best is yet to come!

I hope that as a teacher I can be like the *owner of a house who brings out of his storeroom new treasures as well as old.*[9] For those who have read other literature I have written, some of the contents may seem familiar. About half of this book consists of revisions from previous books.[10] I have divided the book into three main sections. The first section, "What is the Church?" deals with proper concepts of the church. The first three chapters are expanded from my booklet, *Unrealistic Expectations of the Body of Christ*, probably the most popular message I have written (and one that was once printed in a shorter version in *Decision* magazine[11]).

The second section deals with "Leadership in the Church" – emphasizing the need for the right kind of leadership. The third section is more practical, "The Functioning Church."

In all my writing I place Scripture quotations in *italics*, so that the reader can quickly distinguish the words of God from the words of man. (The only exceptions are a few places where italics are used for emphasis.)

My deepest thanks to seven brethren who assisted in editing this book – David Hare, James Garrett, Owen Carey, John Morrison, Lucas and Cherie' Morel, and my dear wife, Teresa. I could never refine a manuscript without such excellent help!

I always encourage those who read my literature to *test everything. Hold on to the good. . . .*[12] If any facets of truth concerning building on the foundation of Jesus Christ spark something good in your spirit, then my goal has been accomplished.

As we study this important subject, join me in prayer.

Lord, we don't know our own hearts.
So search us by the Holy Spirit. Reveal anything offensive to you.
Help us to build upon the foundation of Jesus Christ.
Lord, we don't want to waste our years, to have our life's labor burned up at the judgment seat, and to lose our reward.
So teach us, O God, to build your way and to hear your voice.
Help us to discern; to test all things and hold fast to what is good.
Most of all, may our lives be constantly changed in such a way that we would glorify your name and fully serve your purpose in our generation. In Jesus' name, Amen!

Church Life:

Building on the Foundation of Jesus Christ

SECTION ONE

WHAT IS THE CHURCH?

Chapter One

The Church is the Dwelling Place of God, not an Entertainment Center

When God came to earth, His primary purpose was not just to "save" man; He has always desired to have a people with whom he could dwell: *the Word became flesh and dwelt among us.*[1] The Greek word for *dwell* in the above verse actually means *tabernacled.* In other words, God desires to pitch His tent with us! This truth was stated long ago when God gave His law to Moses:

> *Moreover, I will make my dwelling among you and My soul will not reject you. I will also walk among you and be your God, and you shall be My people.*[2]

Suppose a man had invested much time and expense in building an extravagant and beautiful house for his family. Then one day the house catches on fire and the fire department is quickly called. After the fire truck comes, puts out the fire, and saves the house, the owner will still have his house, but is this the purpose he desired for the house? No! A house is intended to be a dwelling place. A dwelling place is what God is after. Certainly salvation from an eternity in hell is part of God's plan, but it is not His full purpose.

It is also one thing to be a visitor in a house and quite another thing to feel completely at home in a house. When I feel completely at home (in my own house) I can kick off my shoes, rearrange furniture, and look in any closet I please. If I am visiting in a house, however, I do not feel freedom to do any of those things. If this matter of the indwelling Christ were not a necessity in the lives of believers, the apostle Paul would not have prayed as he did:

> . . . that He would grant to you . . . to be strengthened through the Spirit in the inward man, that Christ might finally settle down and feel completely at home in your hearts . . .[3]

We see from beginning to end in the Bible God's desire to dwell among us. In the Old Covenant, God chose Zion, the Jewish people, because he desired them *for his dwelling.*[4] Anytime we study the tabernacle or the temple, we can easily get sidetracked by all the details and miss the primary truth. God has always wanted a dwelling place among His people.

"I will make my dwelling among you . . ."

16

The tabernacle was centered right in the midst of God's people as they traveled through the wilderness. God does not want to be on the outskirts; he wants to be right in our midst! Solomon's temple was never intended to be a grand cathedral in which God's people would meet; rather, it was to be the "house of God," a reminder that God desired to dwell among his people.

What seems to be the primary purpose for God's people in the New Covenant? Is it to make us a successful, religious organization? Is it to make us a group of prosperous and healthy individuals? Is it to be an entertainment center which tries to keep Christians happy? No, rather, His called-out-ones are first and foremost intended to be the home of God; we are *being built together to become a dwelling in which God lives by his Spirit.*[5] In the final chapters of God's record, we see His ultimate desire for His people, His bride, the New Jerusalem:

> *And I heard a loud voice from the throne saying, "Now the dwelling of God is with men, and he will live with them. They will be his people, and God himself will be with them and be their God.*[6]

As Jesus began his ministry, two disciples who encountered his call on their lives, asked him the right question, *"Rabbi . . . where are you staying?"*[7] or as the King James Version asks, *"Where dwellest thou?"* This is the question every follower of Jesus should be asking, "Lord, where are you dwelling?" A contemporary Christian song says, "Lord, I just want to be where you are . . ." This ought to be the desire of our hearts. King David expressed this priority when he said,

> *I will allow no sleep to my eyes,*
> *no slumber to my eyelids,*
> *till I find a place for the LORD,*
> *a dwelling for the Mighty One of Jacob.*[8]

What is the Church's Primary Attraction?

We make a dreadful mistake if, in order to keep members, we need to provide a certain measure of entertainment. Churches sometimes take desperate measures to draw people. One pastor of a church of 5,000, said, "We want the church to look like a mall. We want you to come in here and say, 'Dude, where's the cinema?'" Another church placed an ad in its large city newspaper. The ad boasted that the church was that city's "best kept secret." It listed ten reasons people should visit the church. Among them was "You will have more fun than you thought was legal in church;" "Every service is a PARTY!" "You can be yourself!" "The music rocks!" "It ain't boring!" In the ten reasons listed the only mention of Jesus was "Jesus will be there . . . in jeans!" One new believer told me he visited the church but quit going because it reminded him too much of nightclubs he used to hang out in before he was saved. A. W. Tozer once stated, "It is scarcely possible in most places to get anyone to attend a meeting where the only attraction is God."[9]

Some churches feel that a "full program" is essential; that with the right combination of seminars, retreats, movies, outside speakers, and contemporary singing groups, most churches could probably expect an increase in membership, possibly even doubling in size. Some churches, warns Charles Colson, are in danger of becoming nothing more than "places where people go for their one-hour a week inspirational fix."[10]

It might be wisdom in any church to limit the number of outside speakers, seminars and movies in order to discourage people from thinking of Christianity as a spectator sport. We should also seek to avoid contributing to the busyness that is already a problem with many people.

Seminars and conventions can be a help or a hindrance. If overdone, they can distract us from our primary calling and relationship to God. Os Guinness recently pointed out that a generation characterized by "convictions" is usually followed by one of "conventions." Stuart Briscoe adds his concern about the multitude of seminars that are readily available to us:

> Perhaps I am overly critical, but I suspect that the Church may be catering to people's reluctance to do things by putting on innumerable seminars and training sessions to teach them how to do them. By the time the people have attended all the seminars, they can legitimately say that they don't have the time to do anything about the things they learned in the seminar. And by the time they have explained that point, it's time to go to the next seminar![11]

In summary, may we seek above all else to be the dwelling place of God. The Lord's primary calling for the church is not to serve our own needs or even to serve the needs of others. His call is for us to be *a people for God's own possession.*[12] Let us invite the Lord into our own lives and into the corporate life of the church. May we earnestly desire that our local church would become *a dwelling in which God lives by his Spirit.*

Chapter Two
The Church is a Family,
Not a Grocery Store

Someone has said, "The church is not a grocery store where the elders maintain full shelves to keep the people happy." In a grocery store we select what we want; in a family we take the good with the bad. Ern Baxter comments:

> The subnormal understanding of the nature of church has in many instances caused it to deteriorate into a kind of religious social club where many people feel a freedom to come and go as they please. This practice is not entirely valid because, when widespread, it turns the church of God into little more than a lecture hall where people come, in essence, to hear ideas preached.[1]

God wants the local church to be like a family. Scripture says, *Now you are no longer strangers to God and foreigners to heaven, but you are members of God's very own family, citizens of God's country, and you belong in God's household with every other Christian.*[2] The church was never intended to be a cold, impersonal institution or a smooth-operating business. For those who have never been part of a normal, loving family, the church ought to provide some of that same love and acceptance that every person basically needs. The Bible says, *God sets the lonely in families . . .*[3]

21

In God's family, every believer has at least one thing in common – we have the same Elder Brother. It is a most wonderful thought that Jesus calls me his *brother*.[4] His corporate people – his church – are called the *brotherhood of believers*.[5] The terms *brother*, *sister*, and *brethren* are used about 250 times in Paul's letters. When we meet fellow believers from varied backgrounds and cultures, we often find an instant kinship with them. I have met a Ugandan brother halfway around the world and within an hour felt an amazing spiritual kinship, all because we have the same Elder Brother. God's eternal plan, from all eternity, is to have a large, loving family! *For those whom God knew before they were, he also ordained to share the likeness of his Son, so that he might be the eldest among a large family of brothers.*[6]

In a loving family, the members do not just attend meetings together. They enjoy each other's company and eat meals together. They also work out problems and sometimes even face painful confrontations. In our families, when something happens that we do not like and "our feathers get ruffled," we do not just pack our bags and move to another family.

Committed to Imperfect People

Marriage has been defined as "two imperfect people (a man and a woman) who are committed to grow together in love." The same concept is true of the church. In the Early Church we see a group that was <u>devoted</u> *to the apostles' teaching, and to fellowship, to the breaking of bread, and to prayer.*[7] These believers knew that God had placed them in a particular body, with all the good and all the bad. Fenelon, a 17th century saint, stated it well:

It should be remembered that even the best of people leave much to be desired, and we must not expect too much . . . Do not allow yourself to turn away from people because of their imperfections . . . I have found that

22

God leaves, even in the most spiritual people, certain weaknesses which seem to be entirely out of place.[8]

One chief reason we fail in our commitment is because we realize how imperfect our brethren are. We may be too proud to give our lives away to people who are not perfect. So, like Judas, we make only a partial commitment to the body of believers to which we belong, and in our hearts we are aloof. If this is the case, we will usually be the first to criticize those who fall beneath our standards. Stuart Briscoe spoke of this. "Perfection is what people expect of you and that's tough. Generally, they don't expect it of themselves; they expect it of other people. It's an unrealistic expectation."[9]

To be committed to a body of believers is risky; it can result in personal hurts and misunderstandings. The body, however, is something we all need—even with its apparent weaknesses. I have realized that some members of our church who seem the weakest often contribute in the most beneficial ways.[10]

Spiritual Elitism

The "spiritually elite" are a group who believe they are superior or more highly advanced than average believers. This subtle danger is common to fellowship groups who are seeking the Lord, and it will often bring much trouble and divide the body.

Within a local church, a group of believers may have a healthy motivation for all of God's will to be accomplished. They may desire to stand strong in the midst of religious mediocrity. Some lukewarm churches have a remnant group who hold fast to the word of God and encourage the rest to do so, too. These believers may act properly and lovingly challenge the church to higher attainment. A remnant group, however, will often have a tendency to fall into spiritual pride. This is a danger that faces any earnest, zealous follower of Jesus. The following are some attitudes that will indicate we are slipping into a mentality of elitism:

1. Those who consider themselves spiritually elite may have a condescending attitude toward other believers.

We cannot say to other believers, *"I don't need you!"*[11] We must accept every other blood-washed believer as a child of God, a brother or sister in the faith, and a joint heir of God's promises in eternity. In this sense, none of us has an exclusive relationship with God: *Anybody who is convinced that he belongs to Christ should go on to reflect that we belong to Christ no less than he does.*[12]

It is nothing less than religious pride that says, *"God, I thank Thee that I am not like other people."*[13] A condescending attitude is probably one of the ugliest things that can be found in the life of one who calls himself a Christian. Watchman Nee, in writing to believers who were involved in the work of the gospel, stated his concern:

> Some have the habit of looking down upon those who are supposedly inferior and looking up to those who are supposedly superior. It will be a most shameful thing if such a habit is found among God's servants. . . . We cannot serve the Lord if we fail to have this deficiency solved.[14]

If we see things differently from the believers we associate with, or feel we are "further along" than those who are "dragging their feet" spiritually, we must be careful not to look down upon those other servants of God.

> *After all, who are you to criticize the servant of somebody else, especially when that somebody else is God? . . . Why try to make him look small? We shall all be judged one day, not by one another's standards or even our own, but by the standard of Christ.*[15]

24

2. Those who consider themselves spiritually elite may have an attitude of "we are the overcomers."

God certainly has "overcomers" in most congregations – those believers who keep the right priorities in the midst of distractions or those who endure great suffering and keep a shining testimony in the midst of it.[16] Overcomers will avoid compromise and challenge believers to a deeper faith, purity of character and excellence in service. True overcomers, however, will also be those who have humility and know the working of the cross. They will not think of themselves as overcomers; they will simply walk out the reality of that expression. They will have the same spirit as Moses, who experienced the presence and power of God in a unique and powerful way, and yet *he was not aware that his face was radiant.*[17] Overcomers will be those whose "right hand does not know what their left hand is doing." They will have little pride in their own attainment and will realize they have only come so far by the grace of God.

Those who are truly overcomers will not be exclusive in their relationships. They will not limit their fellowship with a small circle of other like-minded "overcomers." Scripture says, *Don't become snobbish, but take a real interest in ordinary people.*[18]

3. Those who consider themselves spiritually elite may have a low level of toleration for the imperfect.

Sometimes people who are morally upright show very little tolerance for those who are struggling with sin or not living up to their standards. This is not to say we should close our eyes to blatant sin or refuse to deal scripturally with matters that need attention in the body of Christ. However, if we realize our own imperfections, it will cause us to be much more gracious toward others. Oswald Chambers once stated, "I am so amazed that God has altered me that I can never despair of anybody."[19] Likewise, Fenelon wrote, "If there is one mark of perfection, it is simply that it can tolerate the imperfections of others."[20]

25

Those who are mature and spiritually strong will be able to hold on to their "heavenly vision" and yet at the same time bear with the failings of the weak.[21] The strong in the faith will not frown on the struggling or show disgust when God's people fail. They will realize they could fail just as easily (if not worse) except for the grace of God.

How should those who are spiritual respond to immaturity and fleshly failings? God's way is to respond in the Spirit, as Derek Prince expressed in one of my favorite quotes:

> There are two things: the actual and the ideal.
> To be mature is to see the ideal and live with the actual.
> To fail is to accept the actual and reject the ideal.
> To accept only that which is ideal and refuse the actual is to be immature.
> Do not criticize the actual because you have seen the ideal;
> Do not reject the ideal because you have seen the actual.
> Maturity is to live with the actual but hold on to the ideal.[22]

Spectators or Participators?

The New Testament emphasis is that all believers, not just a select few, are part of a royal priesthood.[23] Sometimes a pastor is reluctant to share in ministry with others (especially counseling and Sunday morning preaching), thereby keeping the focus of the membership solely upon himself. Members may be discouraged from looking to anyone else for spiritual help. The focus is on this one man—the pastor; if anything good happens in the church, it is credited to him. Likewise, if anything bad happens, it is also credited to him. This can be an unhealthy situation which will diminish any sense of the church being like a family. Robert Girard described the problem:

There is thoroughly entrenched in our church life, an unbiblical two-caste system. In this two-caste system there is a clergy caste which is trained, called, paid, and expected to do the ministering. And there is a laity-caste which normally functions as the audience which appreciatively pays for the performance of the clergy—or bitterly criticizes the gaping holes in that performance (and there are always gaping holes).

No one expects much of the lower or laity caste (except "tendance, tithe, and testimony"). And everyone expects too much of the upper or clergy caste (including the clergy themselves!).[24]

Entitlement Mentality

In the Lord's church, the people of God must realize we have a role to play, something to contribute. Because we are a functioning family, we do not just look for others to serve us and criticize them when they fail to meet the need. John Wimber illustrated this point:

After a meeting some years ago, a young man approached me and asked to talk. He was visibly upset with me. He said, "I've tried without success to contact you for two weeks. I've tried to get help from the church for this guy that I found sitting on the side of the road two weeks ago. He was wet, cold, hungry. I fed him, clothed him, and took him in for the night. I thought the church could take over the next day. But when I called, the staff said they couldn't take him in! I've been caring for him for two weeks. You say you believe the church should care for the poor, but you wouldn't take this man. Why isn't the church caring for this man?"

My response was simple: "The church is caring for this man."

He stared at me for a moment and said, "Ah, but I wanted you to do it."

"Yes, but Jesus wanted you to do it. And you did."[25]

Like the young man, how many times have we pointed some needy person to a pastor or a "more capable" person and, therefore, possibly shirked a God-given appointment for us?

We are living in a society that feels entitled to the best of everything. We hear it all the time:

"You deserve a break today . . ."

"The government ought to be doing more . . ."

"Buy now, pay later . . ."

"I'm looking for the church which can meet my needs . . ."

Bill Hull, in his book, *Building High Commitment in a Low-Commitment World*, speaks out about the entitlement mentality that has crept into the church. Because of the importance of his comments to the present discussion, a lengthy quote is included here.

> *The Entitlement Mentality.* In the church this same spirit manifests itself in the great evangelical adventure, "looking for the church God has for us" or "shopping for a church." I am all for people prayerfully attempting to locate the best church for them. However, I believe the decision should be a bit different from choosing your entrée at a cafeteria. When I was a pastor, I was frequently asked, "What will your church do for me?" "How do you plan to keep my son safe from evil?" "Will we feel good here?" "Is there spiritual warmth?"
>
> *My Kids Deserve the Best.* How many families have decided whether or not to attend a church solely on

the existence of a youth program that will meet the needs of their children? Many a frustrated small church pastor has lost good people who like everything about his church and could make a valuable contribution. Yet they choose a larger church with a full-time youth minister or exciting appendage. The question that freezes most pastors in their tracks is, "Shouldn't my kids come first? I only have them for a short time, and in days like these, they need every help we can get to keep them with the Lord."

I would answer *no!* My kids don't come first; my family does. The most important factor in a child's spiritual development is the parents' spiritual development. Peer relationships are important and so are alternative social and recreational opportunities to counteract the secular options. But it is absolutely foolish for parents to sacrifice their opportunity and challenge to grow just for a youth program that appears to be better.

The "best" may mean pioneering a youth work. Churches across America desperately need a family or two to say, "We will take on the task of starting a healthy youth work." This actually has much more potential to build teens' Christian character than the majority of self-serving, fun-oriented youth works.

In many cases church choice means simply doing what the kids want. That is no way to run a family, make decisions, or train children. Looking for the full-service youth program that appears to be the most fun is part of the entitlement mentality that has thoroughly saturated our evangelical church culture. It is quite rare to find a family or person who approaches the church asking, "How can I serve? What can I do to help?"[26]

I once heard a visitor attending one of our Sunday meetings say he was "shopping around" for the right church. His attitude reminded me of today's sports world, in which "free agency" enables many athletes to "shop around" for the team they like. Sadly, too many Christians today have become "free agents." They have no sense of commitment to a church family, and if something goes wrong in the life of the church, they just "shop around" for a church which will offer them the best package deal.

May the Lord help us to be a loving church family. In any well-adjusted family, the members must look out for one another and be committed in good times and bad. If members have a selfless, caring, servant attitude, it will have a significant impact on that family. This is true for the family of God as well.

Chapter Three

The Church is an Equipping Center, Not a Sympathy Club

The local church should be a place of refuge where the hurting and wounded can come, feel accepted, and receive the healing they need. One of the main ministries of the Holy Spirit is to bring comfort. The Greek idea of "comfort," however, goes beyond just mere sympathy or consolation. It means to encourage, to make strong, and to fortify. In his study of New Testament words, William Barclay points out that the function of the Holy Spirit is to fill a man with the spirit of power and courage which would make him able to cope triumphantly with life. He says the Greek word, *parakalein*, was used for "exhorting troops who are about to go into battle . . . it is the word of the rallying-call to urge fearful and timorous and hesitant soldiers into battle . . . to make a very ordinary man cope gallantly with a perilous and dangerous situation."[1] John Miller, in *Outgrowing the Ingrown Church*, wrote: "The local church was intended by Jesus to be a gathering of people full of faith, strong in their confidence in Him—not a gathering of religious folk who desperately need reassurance."[2] I have known believers who have spent their entire adult life *getting over past hurts*. Such persons have kept their attention too long in the wrong place – themselves! Indeed, the body of Christ must take time to help the wounded in our midst and yet at the same time maintain the goal of equipping them for a life of discipleship – denying themselves daily and following Christ.

31

Over the years, I have known people who have left a particular church because they did not feel loved or because they felt that proper attention was not given them. Sometimes God has used such people to point out deficiencies in our churches. But while we are called to encourage everyone and especially to help the *weak in the faith*,[3] we are not called to be spiritual baby-sitters. When my two sons were little, I would hold their hands when we walked together, especially when crossing dangerous intersections. When they grew up to be teenagers, I no longer held their hands; they could walk on their own, and I expected them to take responsibility for crossing the street safely.

Not a Place to Continue Our Selfish Pursuit of Life

The church is a place where God wants to conform us into his image.[4] It is not a place to continue our selfish pursuit of life. The church leadership has a primary role: to *equip us for service*.[5] The church should be like a "spiritual boot camp," preparing us for warfare, to *endure hardship . . . like a good soldier of Christ Jesus*.[6] Jean Vanier commented:

> Christian communities . . . are not hiding places for the emotions, offering spiritual drugs to stave off the sadness of everyday life. They are not places where people can go to salve their consciences and retreat from reality into a world of dreams. They are places of resource, which are there to help people grow towards freedom, so that they can love as Jesus loves them. "There is no greater love than to give one's life for one's friends."[7]

Some people in our churches will tend to focus too much on themselves and their problems. This is a significant problem in the body of Christ, and it becomes evident when one looks at the best selling Christian books – most of them have to do with solving personal problems, e.g., fixing marriages, healing hurts, solving financial problems, losing weight, or feeling better about one's self. It is true that the Lord will save and bring into our assemblies many hurting people who will carry over into their Christian lives the baggage of the past. These folks will need special attention from members who are sound and stronger in the Lord. Some problems will need long-term care that will require much patience and forbearance from the brethren. However, people's problems must never dominate a local fellowship. When Jesus calls a man to follow Him, he calls him to *deny himself*.[8] This is a call for every believer; there are no exceptions for wounded people. The Amplified Bible says here, *If any one intends to come after Me let him . . . lose sight of himself and his own interests.*

The people of God are not called to be a spiritual problem-solving group, but rather the body of Christ that will encourage people in their relationship with God. Our primary focus should always be on Christ Himself. We will not be able to solve everyone's problems, but we can put their hand into the hand of Jesus. Our greatest command is to *love the Lord your God with all your heart and with all your soul and with all your mind.*[9]

Some people in conversations will only talk of *their* problems, *their* opinions, and *their* concerns for others. These same folks may then wonder why they have a hard time making friends and experiencing joy in life. Scripture says, *A fool finds no pleasure in understanding, but only in airing his own opinions.*[10]

Whenever a group feels compelled to solve everyone's problems, they fail to be an equipping center, preparing people to live a God-centered, rather than a self-centered life. People must be encouraged to begin to look more outward: *Each of you should not only look to your own interests, but also to the interests of others.*[11] Larry Crabb, a respected Christian counselor who has talked with thousands of Christians in need, made this observation:

The Christian life cannot develop without a deepening awareness of what we first recognized at the time of our conversion: self-centeredness still runs deep within us. . . . Self-centeredness convincingly and continually whispers to me that nothing in this universe is more important than my need to be accepted and respectfully treated. Nothing is more necessary to understand than my neediness, in all its complexity and depth. If people were really moral, murmurs self, then everyone who crosses my path, whether shop-keeper, pastor, or spouse, would devote their resources to making me whole, happy, and comfortable.[12]

People who come into our assemblies weighed down by problems must be encouraged first to seek the Lord, instead of attaching themselves to caring Christians as the source of their hope and security: *But seek first his kingdom and his righteousness, and all these things will be given to you as well.*[13] Frequently when I counsel people with personal problems, I will ask, "How is your personal time with the Lord? Are you spending much time in the word and prayer?" Almost always, their answer is in the negative. If people who have serious financial problems would take the first step mentioned above and *seek first His kingdom*, then things would more likely begin to fall into place. The truth of the matter, sad to say, is that many people simply will not pray or seek the Lord for His help. If this is the case, we must still show grace and love them with the boundless love of Jesus. We must not, however, allow such self-focused people to distract us from God's plans and priorities for the assembly.

Should We Help Everyone?

The early Christians did not try to meet everyone's needs. When dealing with the practical needs of widows, Paul did not encourage unqualified support for *all* widows; rather, he suggested several practical stipulations—the widow must be over 60 years of age, faithful to her husband, a doer of good deeds, and without supporting relatives.[14] We will not be able to help all people who come to us, and we should not feel guilty when we do not. I frequently get phone calls from people who are simply going down the list of churches in a phone book asking for money. I try to be discerning, but rarely help. I do not get distracted by such calls. Many of these needy people only want a "quick fix;" they do not want the larger solutions to their problems.

People do need flesh-and-blood involvement and reassurance; however, many who come to our churches will become disappointed or disgruntled because they are not coming primarily to seek the Lord Himself and his plan for their lives. Dietrich Bonhoeffer explains:

> Many people seek fellowship because they are afraid to be alone. Because they cannot stand loneliness, they are driven to seek the company of other people. There are Christians, too, who cannot endure being alone, who have had some bad experiences with themselves, who hope they will gain some help in association with others. They are generally disappointed. Then they blame the fellowship for what is really their own fault. The Christian community is not a spiritual sanatorium.[15]

Christians must always balance compassion with discernment. Just because we see a need does not mean God is personally calling us to respond. Joseph Stowell, former President of Moody Bible Institute, wrote these words of wisdom to Christian leaders:

> Some of our parishioners are like bottomless buckets. We pour ourselves into them, feeling like that ought to fill them up – and the next time we look into their

bucket, it's empty again. I finally realized that some people who have problems have them because they learned a long time ago that when they were in difficulty, someone would pay attention to them and they would feel loved and cared for. The "problem" was only a means to an end.

These individuals can never be helped. They will consume your time, possess your energies, and manipulate you. When you tell them you've finally decided that you can no longer help them and try to send them to another counselor you think can help them, they will usually resist, saying they've been to that counselor before or they've tried people like that before and you're the only one who can help them – and that if you don't help them, no one will ever be able to help them. I've even had people tell me that if I wouldn't help them, they were going to commit suicide – the ultimate manipulative stroke to keep their thirst for attention satisfied at the well of our schedule.[16]

We must have a realistic, God-focused attitude toward the unlimited problems some people seem to have. We will often be called to give sacrificial help of our time and resources. However, we must ultimately point people to the Lord and take the attitude of the ancient king who exclaimed, *"If the Lord does not help you, from where shall I help you?"*[17]

Attention on the Head

If we look at a person's natural body our attention is usually drawn to the head. That same focus of attention should be true of the spiritual body. Our main purpose as the body of Christ should be to draw attention to the Lord Jesus Himself. While it is true that a church is a place where personal needs are often met, the complete peace that our souls long for will never be found merely in the fellowship of God's people. True peace can be discovered only in God himself: *Find rest, O my soul, in God alone; My hope comes from him. He alone is my rock and my salvation; He is my fortress, I will not be shaken.*[18] The church should be focused more on God than ourselves. A. B. Simpson once stated: "Whenever the church becomes self-conscious and self-centered, she fails to accomplish her real divine calling. Her highest glory is to be seen only in the revealing of the Lord."[19]

Our churches are pervaded with common complaints. Most of these members' complaints have to do with the lack of attention that is shown them. Some members will complain because people never visit them or invite them into their homes. Others will feel ignored and left out of the "in group." Some members will become upset because the pastor seldom or never visits their homes. The root of this problem is a failure to focus on Christ as the Head of the body. R. J. Rushdoony reproved self-centered thinking:

> No one is called to be a passive Christian, to be courted, waited upon, or soothed by the pastor and church. Passive Christianity is a contradiction in terms. . . . The church is Christ's army. Its purpose is not to provide breakfast in bed for all members, and a social lift for the unsocial, but a faith for life, preparation for battle against the powers of darkness, and a strategy of life for victory. The ineffectiveness of the modern church is partially due to this passivity.[20]

The early Christians were not absorbed in plans and programs to keep everyone happy and interested. These Christians were absorbed with the King, Jesus Christ, and the kingdom that He was establishing in the hearts of men. May this be true for us as well.

Chapter Four

The Church is the Pillar and Support of the Truth

If I am delayed, you will know how people ought to conduct themselves in God's household, which is the church of the living God, the pillar and foundation of the truth.[1]

One characteristic of the church of Jesus Christ is that it is to be a place where truth is found. Many people would think of the church as a place where they find loving friends, worshipful music, great kids' programs, and personal needs met. However, a church excelling in all these things would still be lacking if it was not a place where truth was emphasized.

The church is both the *pillar* and *foundation* of the truth. The word, *pillar,* simply means a "column or support."[2] The word, *foundation,* means a "support," "mainstay," or "that which has been made stable and settled firmly."[3] In other words, the church is the *settled foundation* upon which truth rests and it also is like a *pillar* which supports, or lifts up the truth for all to see.

In the Greek, this passage emphasizes it is *the truth* that we are to be concerned with. This refers to the gospel *truth,* the body of truth related to Jesus and the teaching of the apostles. James Garrett expanded on this idea:

The Church is not concerned with the teaching of philosophers, psychologists, or great thinkers, except as they relate to *the truth*, of which the Church is called to be the pillar and ground. There is much truth concerning many fields of knowledge that the Bible does not address.

Some time ago, I cut down a tree. One of my grandsons, watching me wield the axe, wanted to try it. I had to teach him how. He could have read the Bible eight hours a day and never would he have learned how to use an axe.

When I dug ditches for Muskogee County, as a teenager, the first few hours were very difficult, until a man named, Dick Biggs, said, "Here boy, let me show you how to use your legs to push that shovel." As a teenager, I prayed daily and read the Sermon on the Mount over and over, but that did not teach me how to use a shovel.

One could read the Bible from morning to night and never have an understanding of the valences of chemical elements, or algebra, or computer science. The Church has no business making pronouncements in matters that lie beyond its biblical mandate. There have been sad episodes in Church History when ecclesiastical authorities made dogma their pronouncements in matters in which the Bible is silent or open to interpretation. Only when experts in practical and theoretical disciplines begin to use their expertise as a platform to oppose *the truth*, should the Church get involved in those disciplines. When that happens, it becomes the business of the Church.[4]

It is not an individual, but the corporate church which is God's primary tool for expressing his truth in the world. W. Robertson Nicoll, in his commentary, *The Expositor's Greek*

Testament, commented on the church being the *pillar and support of the truth.*

> The Church . . . is the divinely constituted human Society by which the support and maintenance in the world of revealed truth is conditioned. Truth if revealed to isolated individuals, no matter how numerous, would be dissipated in the world. But the Divine Society in which it is given an objective existence, at once compels the world to take knowledge of it, and assures those who receive the revelation that it is independent of, and external to, themselves, and not a mere fancy of their own.[5]

There are three basic ways that the church is the pillar and support of the truth.

1. The Church must Live out the Truth.

A Scripture is often quoted to encourage believers to be honest with one another: *speaking the truth in love . . .*[6] Preachers often refer to this and encourage us to be sure and have love in our hearts when we are speaking truth to one another. However, this a limited application of this verse. The Greek word means more than just our speech; in the best sense of the word, it means *being truthful,*[7] or *walking in truth.*[8] The Amplified Bible brings out this fuller meaning:

> *Rather, let our lives lovingly express truth [in all things speaking truly, dealing truly, living truly]. Enfolded in love, let us grow up in every way and in all things into Him Who is the Head, [even] Christ . . .*[9]

When we look at the verse before, we see why it is so important for the church to express the truth: *As a result, we are no longer to be children, tossed here and there by waves and carried about by every wind of doctrine, by the trickery of men, by craftiness in deceitful scheming.*[10]

Because there are many *winds of doctrine* and many deceivers in the land, we must not be naive. We must be lovers of the truth. The reason many people are lured into cults is not because of false teaching or demonic influences deceiving them. The ultimate reason is because they have failed to love the truth as it applies to them.

> *They perish because they refused to love the truth and so be saved. For this reason God sends them a powerful delusion so that they will believe the lie . . .*[11]

> *All this disaster has come upon us, yet we have not sought the favor of the Lord our God by turning from our sins and giving attention to your truth.*[12]

Jesus declared that He was *the truth*.[13] If Jesus is living inside us, then our lives should exemplify something of his truth. Jesus was God's truth incarnate – where mankind could see divine thought in flesh-and-blood. God's truth is not just a chapter in a philosophy book or a lofty concept for religious discussion groups. God's truth – his Word – was made flesh:

> *The Word became flesh and made his dwelling among us. We have seen his glory, the glory of the One and Only, who came from the Father, full of grace and truth.*[14] *That which was from the beginning, which we have heard, which we have seen with our eyes, which we have looked at and our hands have touched – this we proclaim concerning the Word of life.*[15]

Jesus came *full of grace and truth* and we – his representatives on the earth – should likewise be *full of grace and truth*. The Revised

English Bible translates the last sentence of the Scripture above as follows: *Our theme is the Word which gives life.*[16] Could people say this is the theme of our church?

2. The Church must Teach the Truth.

I once heard a message which had a short passage of Scripture read at the beginning followed with about forty minutes of the speaker's humor. The crowd was excited and laughing hilariously throughout the message. This man who had a reputation for a "teaching ministry," actually did very little teaching. At the end of the message I had to ask, "What was really accomplished by this message?" Was the church strengthened in faith? Encouraged for life? Challenged in personal convictions?

What were Jesus' final words – his Great Commission to his followers? To preach the gospel and to save souls? That is a partial answer; but, it is also a universal summons *to make disciples . . . teaching them to obey everything I have commanded you.*[17] We are urged not to be selfish with what we have learned, but to take the treasure of truth that has been freely given us and entrust it to others. *Guard . . . the treasure which has been entrusted to you . . . and these entrust to faithful men who will be able to teach others also.*[18] Teaching the word of God is therefore a responsibility of every believer.

In the church of Jesus Christ, good teaching can be found. But, sometimes teaching is distorted in its content or even neglected entirely. In churches across the land, godly teaching has frequently been replaced by lovely sermons which keep emotions pleasantly satisfied, yet leave souls spiritually empty. At the other extreme is teaching which has become too academic with overemphasis on correct, systematic Biblical knowledge. This feeds intellectual craving and curiosity, but there is little substance to produce changed character and fruitful lives for the glory of God. The body of Christ needs to rediscover proper teaching for the local assembly and for the individual disciple.

Teaching was a major part of Jesus' work on this earth. Of all his ministries (e.g., evangelism, healing, visiting, etc.) teaching stands out foremost. Of the ninety times Jesus was addressed in the Gospels, sixty times he was called *Rabbi*, which means *Teacher*. However, the way Jesus related truth and the way we relate it today are often far apart.

Every Christian disciple is called to a certain measure of teaching. Some believers will have a gift of teaching and they will have a greater responsibility before the Lord: *we who teach will be judged more strictly*.[19] A person who has been gifted by God to teach the word will need to exhibit in his life a good measure of what he publicly proclaims. He should not be slack in his devotion to the word of God and to prayer. The one called to teaching must unreservedly embrace the responsibilities of his ministry: *If our gift is . . . teaching, let us give all we have to our teaching*.[20]

Teaching was a vital part of the early church and should be so today. It is recorded in Acts that *the apostles never stopped teaching*[21] and the believers *met constantly to hear the apostles teach*.[22] Throughout the history of the church, there have been good teachers as well as bad. I have written another book which deals more in detail with practical matters related to teaching.[23]

There are some who teach, but have no business doing so. Scripture warns against those who *teach false doctrines . . . who promote controversies rather than God's work . . . who turn to meaningless talk . . . who want to be teachers . . . but they do not know what they are talking about or what they so confidently affirm*.[24] The need today is not just for more teachers, but for more of the right kind of teachers. There are many who do not seek sound truth that will transform the innermost being; instead they *gather around them a great number of teachers to say what their itching ears want to hear*.[25] Far too many teachers today are catering to the whims of people, rather than carefully handling the oracles of God.

3. The Church must Share the Truth With an Unsaved World.

In an Old Testament story, four desperate lepers, during a time of severe famine, discover an empty Aramean camp, because the Lord caused the Aramean soldiers to hear a sound of a great army and they left suddenly. In this camp there are all kinds of food, clothing, and money. As they start enjoying their newly found treasure, it suddenly dawns on them that their fellow-Israelites back in their own city are still starving.

> *Finally, they said to each other, "This is not right. This is wonderful news, and we aren't sharing it with anyone! If we wait until morning, some terrible calamity will certainly fall upon us. Come on, let's go back and tell the people at the palace."*[26]

The lesson we can learn from this story is that we who are believers have likewise found a great treasure – Christ! It just *is not right* if we keep this wonderful truth all to ourselves. It is the will of God to bring the knowledge of his truth to all men. *This is good, and pleases God our Savior, who wants all men to be saved and to come to a knowledge of the truth.*[27]

It is easy to forget that a central reason Jesus came to this earth was to seek and to save what was lost.[28] Jesus told the parable of a shepherd who left ninety-nine sheep in the open country and went after the one lost sheep until he found it and returned with great joy.[29] We sometimes forget the words to the hymn: "I once was lost, but now am found . . ." Did not our Lord pursue us and show us his amazing grace? Where would we be today had he not taken initiative in revealing His incredible truth and mercy to us, who were so undeserving? Yet, do we not grow comfortable in the midst of our Christian friendships and activities and end up spending little, if any, time with the lost? Do we have any desire for our neighbors to *be saved and to come to a knowledge of the truth?* Donald McGavarn, who has done quite a bit of research on churches, reproved our current status: "Far too many congregations and denominations, facing the most responsive world ever to exist, are spending 85–99 percent of their time, prayer, money, and thought in looking after themselves."[30]

Why do we not spend more time on those who do not know Christ? Lack of compassion, busyness with our own affairs, and the threat of rejection may be reasons for this negligence, but there may be a deeper root. Watchman Nee explained in an intimate letter written to believers with whom he was associated: "At present I have a very deep conviction, and that is that God's children lack a living experience of Christ. As a consequence, they are not willing to spend energy and money on sinners.[31]

The closer we get to Christ, the closer we will share His heart, which longs for a dying and lost world to come to Him.

We are living in a generation which emphasizes relativism – that there is no absolute truth. That what is true for one might be fine, but what is true for another might be something else. That what is true today might not be true tomorrow. Statistics from one pollster George Barna showed that in 2001, only twenty-two percent of the general public believed there was "absolute truth, i.e., that there are moral truths or principles which do not change according to the circumstances."[32] Sad to say, the same poll showed among professing "born again" believers that only thirty- two percent said they believed in absolute truth. If this is true, it would mean more than two-thirds of professing believers today do not believe in absolute truth! Indeed, the church has quite a responsibility to be *the pillar and foundation of the truth.*

If a local church fails to emphasize sharing truth with the lost and settles for transfer growth (members switching churches), the group will certainly suffer. God intended our focus to be outward as well as inward. When we look at biblical metaphors of the church – *salt, light, ambassadors, branches, army, and pilgrims* – they all denote movement and outward orientation.

T. Austin-Sparks, a man who knew the deep things of God, realized that two things must be kept in balance – evangelism (reaching the lost) and edification (building up believers). If one of these were missing, he believed imbalance would result:

> If building up is given a place out of all proportion to evangelism, we shall have another malformation. There will arise an ultra-spirituality which is divorced from what is practical. Truth will – sooner or later – take the place of Life. The mental will rule out the truly spiritual. The worst outcome will be that those involved will be found to have come into a false position which will not stand up to the tests of real life. . . . For the real proof of spiritual life is in its ability to express Christ in love, forbearance, patience, meekness, and self-forgetfulness, in an unsympathetic, misunderstanding, and unappreciative world. This does not mean that there should be a limiting of either evangelism or building up, but it does mean that there must be a close relationship between the two.[33]

An outward focus is essential to the health of a local fellowship. How many times have we known a couple who has just had their first baby to have a "newness" in their lives? Things are no longer focused inwardly – on just themselves – but suddenly they have to devote a lot of time, energy, and expense on this new addition! Having a baby is a healthy thing for a couple; and this is also true of "spiritual babies" in the church. When a person gets saved and comes into a local assembly, he will have plenty of questions that need answering and maybe even some "messes" that need cleaning. Babies require an enormous amount of love, care, protection, and feeding. However, a newborn soul will bring new life and health into any assembly. We are missing something when we are lacking "spiritual babies."

May the Lord give us more of His compassion for the lost: *He is not wanting anyone to perish, but everyone to come to repentance.*[34] A highly organized evangelistic strategy is not needed if we all are sensitive to the Holy Spirit in planting spiritual seeds or watering where another man has already planted. We need to be willing to be bold and to be rejected at times. Sometimes, practical deeds done by Christians will open up opportunities to speak of Christ. We will not always immediately win people, but if we can lead a person one inch closer to Jesus, we will have accomplished something. Every believer and every local church should earnestly desire to extend the mercy and truth of God to needy souls for whom Christ died.

Let us never forget the awesome task the Master has entrusted to us – his church – to be the *pillar and support of the truth.* May we walk faithfully in the truth – living it out personally, speaking it when granted opportunities, teaching it to hungry disciples, and sharing it in all the world.

SECTION TWO

LEADERSHIP IN THE CHURCH

Chapter Five
Shared Leadership

In the past several years, I have heard three different lectures about "ministerial burnout." In these talks, a variety of reasons for burnout were given, but I was surprised that none of the speakers mentioned what would seem to be a major factor: is it possible that many pastors are doing a job which God never intended for one man to do? And, never mentioned was the possibility of a shared leadership as a solution for this common problem in the body of Christ.

One pastor candidly described how he got caught up in running a "one-man-show."

> Assuming leadership as pastor of a church put me in position to do it all. I picked up people in my car to bring them to church, then led the singing, made the announcements, performed the musical solos and specials, preached the message, prophesied over the congregation, laid hands on them, and blessed them. Then I took them home. At the end of the day, I fell into bed totally fatigued but contented. All this for a grand total of 30 to 40 people. This foolish heart had so much to learn. Church is for the cultivating and developing of gifts, talents, and ministries. It is not meant to be a "one-man-show" in which one person puts on a performance while everyone else fills the role of spectator.[1]

Our Story in Staunton

Having a plurality of leaders is not always easy, but the advantages are worth considering. For the past thirty-five years, our church in Staunton, Virginia—Community Fellowship Church—has operated under shared leadership. The relationship between several elders/pastors has been a healthy thing for us and for the congregation we oversee. Our church had its beginnings in the home of Paul Knopp, a former Church of God pastor, who decided to invite family and some friends for informal meetings. Before long, more than fifty people were gathering and it seemed God was raising up a church. In those days Paul refused suggestions that he become "the pastor." He was emphatic, "This will not be *my* church; it will be the Lord's. I will help out in oversight, but I will not be the sole leader." One reason Paul felt this way was that he knew his gifts were limited and a growing body would need other leaders. Within a few months, a local college professor and a college student, who were both leading Bible studies on their respective campuses, began to attend. Over some time, it became apparent they possessed needed qualities of leadership, and we had our first three elders. It seemed obvious to all that *the Holy Spirit* had set these men as overseers in the body (Acts 20:28). Over the years, our eldership has changed as some have moved away and others have been raised up within the local church. We have never had to send away for a leader.

Advantages of Shared Leadership

(1) Shared leadership distributes the burden of oversight. Jethro's words to Moses are still applicable to many pastors today: *What you are doing is not good. You and these people who come to you will only wear yourselves out. The work is too heavy for you; you cannot handle it alone.*[2] Moses, who had been busy every day from early morning to late evening, solely taking care of people's problems, heeded his father-in-law and appointed other leaders to help share his load. In our current church of about 300 members, we have five elders plus other gifted men who help to share the load. All of us are active, but none of us is burning out.

(2) Shared leadership provides a variety in ministry. Even when there is an associate pastor and a supporting staff, most pastors believe they are responsible for all the Sunday morning preaching/teaching, leading a Wednesday night meeting, and doing most of the counseling. In our eldership we have a variety of men who can minister—one who is gifted more in systematic teaching, one in exhortation, one in encouragement, and one prophetically. Any pastor/elder will have deficiencies, and if other men are involved in leadership, weaknesses will be balanced out. We also try to incorporate other gifted men and women. Through this varied ministry, the body is fed a well-balanced diet. Each week we seek the Lord to know who is to share a message. If more than one has a burden, then we pray until one brother will sense a leading from the Lord, and the other will sense a check in his spirit. If only one of these men, though quite gifted, were to do most of the public ministry, the body would suffer: *If everything were concentrated in one part, how could there be a body at all?*[3]

(3) Shared leadership provides accountability and support for one another. In our eldership we are friends first and co-workers second. We have a close relationship and can therefore be very honest with each other. After one message I delivered, a fellow elder said, "Clay, that message was OK, but I saw too much of you today, and not enough of Jesus." Now, if we did not have the relationship we do, that rebuke would have certainly "ruffled my feathers!" However, my brother saw some pride in me that I was not aware of. I was thankful for the words, even though they were hard to receive.

One of our elders once went through a heart-wrenching divorce and if we had not been there to walk together with him through several tough years, it could have been a disastrous time for him. I know some pastors who do not have even one man in the congregation with whom they can share their personal lives. This is sad, indeed. Though some seminaries teach pastors not to get too close to their congregation, open and accountable relationships are essential, and are the norm in the New Testament.

(4) Shared leadership keeps our attention more on the Head of the body, Jesus Christ. In many a conversation I have asked believers how things are going in their churches. The answer invariably comes back, "Oh, just great! Pastor John [fictitious name] is such a fine man!" How many churches are known as "Pastor John's church?" When one man has full responsibility, he will inadvertently be given some of the glory as well as the blame for what happens. Shared leadership can help keep the focus of the church where it ought to be—on the Lord Himself.

The Biblical Basis for Shared Leadership

In the New Testament three terms denote one and the same role: *pastor* (shepherd), *overseer* (bishop), and *elder* (presbyter). In Acts 20, we see these three synonymous terms all used of the same men.

From Miletus, Paul sent to Ephesus for the <u>elders</u> of the church. Keep watch over yourselves and all the flock of which the Holy Spirit has made you <u>overseers</u>. Be <u>shepherds</u> [pastors] of the church of God, which he bought with his own blood.[4]

The same three terms are also used interchangeably in I Peter 5:

> To the _elders_ among you, I appeal as a fellow elder, a witness of Christ's sufferings and one who also will share in the glory to be revealed: Be _shepherds_ [pastors] of God's flock that is under your care, serving as _overseers_—not because you must, but because you are willing, as God wants you to be; not greedy for money, but eager to serve; not lording it over those entrusted to you, but being examples to the flock. And when the Chief Shepherd appears, you will receive the crown of glory that will never fade away.[5]

Notice the apostle Peter addresses elders in his church as a _fellow-elder_ [Greek – co-elder]. He doesn't refer to himself as a "pastor above elders." There is also no mention of a "senior pastor;" only Jesus is called the _Chief Shepherd_. (Matthew Henry rightly calls our Lord, "the great Pastor of the universe."[6])

The word _pastor_ is only used one time in the New Testament, and it is in the plural (Eph. 4:11). The terms _elders_ and _overseers_ are likewise always used in the plural in the New Testament.

- Acts 11:30 . . . _elders_
- Phil. 1:1 . . . _overseers and deacons_
- Acts 14:23 . . . _when they had appointed elders_
- I Thes. 5:12-13 . . . _those (plural) who have charge_
- Acts 15:2-4 . . . _apostles and elders_
- I Tim. 5:17 . . . _elders who direct the church well_
- Acts 15:6,22,23 . . . _apostles and elders_
- Tit. 1:5 . . . _appoint elders in every city_
- Acts 20:17,28 . . . _elders of the church . . . overseers_
- Heb. 13:7,17,24 . . . _leaders_
- Eph. 4:11 . . . _pastors_
- James 5:14 . . . _call for the elders_
- I Peter 5:1-3 . . . _elders_

The modern day concept of a senior pastor who stands in authority above other church leaders has little biblical basis, as many theologians have noted:

Philip Schaff: "The terms *presbyter* (or elder) and *bishop* (or overseer) denote in the New Testament one and the same office . . . they appear always as a plurality or as a college in one and the same congregation. . . . With the beginning of the second century, from Ignatius onward, the two terms are distinguished and designate two offices."[7]

John Calvin: "In giving the name of bishops, presbyters, and pastors, indiscriminately to those who govern churches, I have done it on the authority of Scripture, which uses the words as synonymous."[8]

J. Rodman Williams: "Elders are shepherds or pastors, and the words signify the same function. We must be on guard against any idea that pastors are other than shepherds . . . Plurality of leadership is the New Testament picture. With neither governing person nor governing body above another, it means that every body of elders is much like the original group of apostles, whose only authority beyond them was the Lord Himself."[9]

Michael Green: "One-man leadership is bad for the man and for the church. The man tends to imagine he has gifts that God has not given him, and that he is nearly indispensable. The members of the congregation see that he thinks that way and find it convenient to go along with it. Even if everything seems to be highly successful while he is in charge, it folds once he is gone."[10]

Wayne Grudem: "Plural elders is the pattern in all New Testament. . . . some have argued that different forms of church government are evident in the New Testament, a survey of relevant texts shows the opposite to be true: there is quite a consistent pattern of *plural elders* as the main governing group in New Testament churches. . . . No passage suggests that any church, no matter how small, had only one elder."[11]

The New Testament does not provide detailed blueprints for church government, so we must be cautious in saying one specific way of government must be *the* way for every church assembly. We must allow the Holy Spirit to work uniquely in each congregation. Even if additional elders are desired, it may take time for good capable men to be raised up for leadership.

Some might make a case for a single pastor in James, who did have a place of prominence in the Jerusalem church. This prominence, however, may have been due to his apostolic stature and the voluntary traveling of others, including Peter. A single pastor who is a good leader and knows Christ intimately may be better than plural leaders who are irresponsible, not gifted in overseeing the flock, or motivated by selfish ambition. The goal of any leadership – whether individual or shared – is to *equip the saints for the work of service*.[12]

Why Shared Leadership is Rare

George Barna, respected Christian researcher, recently wrote a book entitled, *The Power of Team Leadership*, in which he encourages churches to consider a shared leadership. Barna's primary theme is that "Leadership works best when it is provided by teams of gifted leaders serving together in pursuit of a clear and compelling vision."[13] Barna says, however, that in spite of the abundance of compelling reasons to do so, "It is safe to predict that most Protestant churches will not incorporate team leadership into their ministry practices in the foreseeable future."[14] Then he lists the following reasons church leaders are reluctant to embrace a shared leadership:

(1) The desire for simplicity. It's sometimes easier to lead without the encumbrance of other people. In addition, many leaders feel they can do a better job by themselves.

(2) The need for control. Some prefer to dominate rather than rely upon the breadth of experience resident in the congregation.

(3) The need for personal significance. Many leaders fight hard to maintain complete authority, because they have a deep-seated need to be needed.

(4) The quest for efficiency. "I can do it faster myself."

(5) Adherence to tradition. Despite the widespread ridicule of churches' stubborn adherence to outdated traditions and practices, thousands continue to resist reasonable change. It has been said that the seven last words of the church will be, "We've never done it that way."[15]

The unfortunate thing is that many congregations have never even remotely considered a shared leadership, and this may be to their loss. The following are some common objections one might have about plural leaders.

Common Objections

(1) Shared leadership is not practical – you can't run a corporation with 2 or 3 heads. This may be true of a business, but the Lord's church is not to be run like a business. In an eldership, sometimes one brother may be more prominent than others. The apostle Peter called himself a "fellow-elder" and yet I am sure he was prominent in his local fellowship simply because of his spiritual stature and apostolic authority.

Dale Rumble, from Kingston, New York, has been involved for over thirty-five years with churches operating under a shared leadership. In earlier years, Rumble was the only leader in groups he was overseeing, but he purposed to make room for other men to work alongside him. Rumble emphasizes diversity in leadership and says that elders are not necessarily co-equal in stature, ability, visibility or experience. They are simply equal in bearing responsibility for oversight of the congregation. Elders are not clones; they will be different in personality and in the nature of their specific ministry. A good term to describe such elders is "collegial." It connotes more the idea of colleagues – on equal footing. Just as a college has different departments with different heads, each an expert in his particular field, so ideally a plural form of church leadership will include men who are gifted in diverse areas.

This form of leadership requires men who realize their need of additional leadership, and who can defer to one another in a spirit of meekness. Rumble comments about the advantages of shared leadership, "Shared leadership is the proper environment from which to train, disciple, test, and release men into trans-local ministry. There are no disadvantages to shared leadership; only the time and commitment necessary for elders to be trained in character, ministry, servanthood, and accountability. Without humility and a heart to serve, however, it will never work."[16]

(2) Shared leadership encourages passivity since no one wants to take the lead. If elders are in a good working relationship, this will not be a problem. Scripture says, *If you are a leader, exert yourself to lead.*[17] In our fellowship we will not make major decisions without unanimity among elders and positive input from the body. However, each elder feels free in his realm of ministry to initiate whatever he senses the Lord leading. One of our elders, for example, is a principal of a Christian school that is under the oversight of our church eldership. Because this brother is gifted in administration and has a greater vision for Christian education than the rest, we often defer to his judgment in specific school matters, while providing oversight with major policy or personnel decisions.

(3) Shared leadership breeds insecurity. I have heard some say that our form of church government will breed insecurity, because we do not have a senior pastor who holds all things together. One family left our church and when later asked why, the couple replied, "We want to go somewhere where there is a real pastor." If believers derive their security from a sole pastor, it is a false security. Any individual man will have certain characteristics or make certain decisions that will cause members to be disappointed in him. Our security should never be in each other, but only in the Lord Jesus Himself: *Look to me and be saved, all the ends of the earth! For I am God, and there is no other.*[18]

(4) Shared leadership does not work. Some will say, "You do not see churches (especially churches who are booming with members) with this type of leadership." This is not a good argument, because we should never put "what works" as the primary criteria, but "what is biblical?" We are not seeing many miracles in America in our day. Does this mean miracles are not valid just because we are not seeing many? We have not seen a lot of genuine apostles and prophets in our day. Does this mean they are not valid? The church of our day is in a developing stage; we are *being built* together to *become* a dwelling in which God lives by the Spirit.[19] God is in the process of restoring and maturing His church. Some truths about the church have been de-emphasized or ignored in the past, but God is bringing more to light every day. Shared leadership is one such truth, which should be increasingly helpful to the body of Christ in the days ahead as we rediscover its value.

The fact is, across this land and abroad, many congregations have enjoyed the advantages of a shared leadership. I am personally acquainted with a number of congregations who have successfully walked in this truth over a number of years.

One good example is Tulsa Christian Fellowship, birthed in October 1969. The church began when Bill Sanders, pastor of a Southern Baptist Church in Tulsa, was "released" because of his doctrines concerning the Holy Spirit and his interest in evangelizing street hippies. Several members of the church also left and soon a new church was born. Charles Farah Jr., a professor of theology at Oral Roberts University, joined Bill in leadership shortly thereafter. Charles and Bill began studying the Scriptures and desired to see the new church patterned after the New Testament. Elders were chosen but it took some time for the church government to develop, as many members were used to the pastor-led model. For the past twenty years this church has functioned effectively under the leadership of a plurality of elders.

Presently Tulsa Christian Fellowship is led by a plurality of seven elders with a congregation of about 300. All seven elders preach regularly. Four receive some financial support from the church, two of these receive full time support. No one elder is the "senior elder." Each elder tends to be the primary leader when the agenda is in the arena of his personal gifts and experience. One elder, for example, has more of a burden and oversight of small groups, so his leadership in that area is often deferred to. Another elder is more gifted in administration, so he is given free rein in his area. The leaders meet every Tuesday morning at 6 A.M. to pray, make decisions, and plan the church life for the week. Decisions are based on consensus, rather than voting. TCF is also a congregation of house-churches, each of which is led by a team of leaders, rather than a single pastor. Some of the house-church leaders also preach on Sunday mornings from time to time.

Jim Garrett, one of the leaders, comments on the advantages they have found from a shared leadership: "For one thing, the congregation is given a full-orbed model of leadership. When there is a single leader, the congregation tends to reflect his gifting, talent, and temperament. Plural preachers/teachers give the congregation a well-rounded spiritual diet, instead of the more restricted diet that comes from a single preacher/teacher. Also, the spiritual burden is shared. When a church member faces a problem that needs pastoral input, the elder who is most gifted in the problem area is available for counsel."[20]

Something to Consider?

Some of my best friends are senior pastors, and I hope our diverse views of church government never hinder our fellowship in Christ. I sometimes wonder, however, if some weary and burdened pastors in the body of Christ would benefit from a shared leadership. Is it possible that much of the frustration and burnout that pastors suffer would be eliminated with a plural leadership structure? Jethro's words to Moses still speak to many pastors: *The work is too heavy for you; you cannot handle it alone.*[21]

One thing is certain: For the average church and pastor to move into a shared leadership will require considerable change and much patience! George Barna comments, "Despite its obvious advantages, for thousands of pastors such a transition is improbable. They were raised to believe that the pastor leads everyone and must have direct, unfettered oversight of the masses. . . . It takes a mature person to embrace team leadership, because it demands giving up the spotlight, the authority, and the view of the pastor as the center of all church activity."[22]

A shared type of leadership may not be the "cure all" for all church problems. Regardless of the particular form of government a church has, however, one man cannot do it alone: *If the whole body were an eye, where would the sense of hearing be? If the whole body were an ear, where would the sense of smell be?*[23] No man should have to bear the burden of church leadership by himself. Shared leadership is a biblical model to consider.

Chapter Six
Desiring More Good Men For Elders

The reason I left you in Crete was that you might straighten out what was left unfinished and appoint elders in every town, as I directed you.[1]

Never be in a hurry about appointing an elder . . .[2]

Once when I was teaching about shared leadership in India, two pastors shared a concern with me: "We are afraid to ordain other elders because sometimes when a pastor has done that, while he is traveling away from the church for a couple weeks, the new elder takes over the church and turns the congregation against him." My response to their concern was twofold: "If that scenario happened then it is quite likely that either (1) the wrong men had been picked as elders or (2) good relationships had not been built in the leadership team."

Appointing good men as elders in the local church ought to be the goal of any leader. In the above verse, Paul implies that there is something *unfinished* in the local church as long as there are no elders. He also said that elders should be appointed in *every* town. During a return visit to churches that they helped to establish, Paul and Barnabas appointed elders for them *in every church.*[3] It is essential, however, that we not be hasty in this important matter and that we seek . . .

The Right Kind of Elders

Here is a trustworthy saying: If anyone sets his heart on being an overseer, he desires a noble task. Now the overseer must be above reproach, the husband of but one wife, temperate, self-controlled, respectable, hospitable, able to teach, not given to drunkenness, not violent but gentle, not quarrelsome, not a lover of money. He must manage his own family well and see that his children obey him with proper respect. (If anyone does not know how to manage his own family, how can he take care of God's church?)[4]

Some excellent chapters have been written by others on qualifications of church elders in this passage, so I will defer to them for the details.[5] In Christendom today, the primary emphasis for qualifying church leaders is academic, but in the biblical pattern, the emphasis is primarily on godly character. As we summarize the above passage, we can say church elders should be:

- Men who love the Lord and are committed to his word.
- Men whose life is above reproach.
- Men who manage their family well and provide for them.
- Men who have a good reputation in the community.

These should be men whom the present leader(s) know(s) personally. Scripture says we should *know those who labor among us.*[6] In our church we look for God to raise up leaders within the body rather than sending away for outside "experts." Whenever we have sensed that God is raising up another elder, we have invited that new man to meet with the elders in our weekly meetings, so we can get to know the man more personally. This process may take extended time. We never feel any pressure to hurry the process. In some cases, either the man himself or our present elders have determined that he would not be suited as an elder.

We do not vote on elders.[7] This was common in the denominational church I grew up in, and usually the elders chosen were the most popular or successful men, but not necessarily the most spiritual men. Scripture says the Holy Spirit sets in overseers.[8] If a present pastor is the sole leader, he and other godly men should determine those who are being raised up as leaders. These will usually be the men who are naturally wanting to teach or preach, who attend the prayer meetings, who are faithful in small things, who display godly character, and who seem to be genuinely concerned for the welfare of church members. They are developing, in general, a shepherd's heart. Our role is simply to recognize what the Holy Spirit is already doing. In our congregation, we do not vote, but we will inform the body that we are considering a particular man for leadership and ask them to pray with us and give any input they might have. We may even teach on the biblical qualifications of elders. We do not look for unanimous approval, but if it is of God, the congregation will confirm His will.

The Church Needs Male Leadership

An overseer, then, must be above reproach, the husband of one wife . . .[9]

Concerning the qualifications for eldership, the New Testament is emphatic – only spiritually and morally qualified men can be elders. Just because a person sincerely wants to help people or aspires to become an elder does not mean he should become one. Only those men who meet God's qualifications can become part of the leadership team in a local church.

Notice in the above verse it does not mention "an overseer . . . must be the wife of one husband . . ." There is no record in the New Testament of any female pastors. Some will be quick to quote Gal 3:28 (*There is neither . . . male nor female, for you are all one in Christ*) and say Paul was dealing with a first century cultural problem – the Jews having an attitude of male superiority. Yet, we must face the facts: the clear biblical pattern is that good and capable men should be elders in the congregation. If we have a problem with male leadership, we ought to consider the following:

- Jesus, the perfect leader, was a man.
- The twelve founding apostles of the church were all men.
- The first seven deacons selected were all godly men.
- The first missionary teams consisted only of men.

While we see that the New Testament pattern is for male leaders, we *do* see much recorded in Scripture about women ministering in the church. Women can certainly be very involved in the work of the kingdom. This has been true throughout the Bible in Jewish history as well as in the history of the Christian church. As the Psalmist says, *The women who proclaim the good tidings are a great host.*[10] The annals of church history record many contributions of bold and spirit-filled women of God who have been the sparkplug of revival and contributed significantly to the growth of the church. The "Bible Women" in the Chinese church are a good illustration of this point:

> Back in the early missionary days, many Chinese women trained in Christian schools and local churches dedicated their lives to Christ's service, and became known as "Bible Women." In those days women in China were very secluded and did not attend public meetings. It was the Bible Women, alongside the lady missionary, who reached them in their homes – visiting the sick, teaching hygiene and child care, and befriending these "inside persons." Later, when such women began attending church, the Bible Women would teach them to read and write, for most were illiterate. They would also be involved in village evangelism.

During the first thirty years under the Communist regime, when so many pastors, evangelists, and leaders were in prison, it was primarily the Bible Women, though no longer called by that name, who stepped into the breach and kept the churches together. Where a Barak is unwilling or not available for that task, God does not hesitate to raise up a Deborah. There are aged "Deborahs" still feeding flourishing churches in China, as in the case of the ninety-year-old who has a congregation of over 500 believers.[11]

Nevertheless, the normal pattern of the New testament emphasizes male leadership. The Bible seems to distinguish between the gospel-related work of a woman and a man. The Scriptures, however, certainly do not forbid public ministry nor narrowly limit a woman's opportunities. The following are some biblically listed ministries for women:

- Evangelism[12]
- Serving/ Deaconess[13]
- Gift of Prophecy[14]
- Hospitality[15]
- Hosting a Prayer Meeting[16]
- Hosting a Church[17]
- Teaching Ministry With Husband[18]
- Teaching Children[19]
- Training Younger Women[20]

As far as opportunities to serve God is concerned, women should never feel slighted!

Should Women Lead and Teach Men?

This is where the controversy dwells, and the following verse is usually at the center of discussion:

A woman should learn in quietness and full submission. I do not permit a woman to teach or to have authority over a man; she must be silent.[21]

First of all, we cannot just toss this verse out as being a cultural problem which does not apply today. If we take that approach, then other teaching in this letter to Timothy about prayer for the government (2:1-4), modesty in dress (2:9-10), qualifications for an elder (Ch. 3), or assisting widows (Ch. 5) could equally have cultural applications and be eliminated. It is important that we understand what Paul is saying, and looking at the Greek text of this passage is a help to our understanding.

It seems that the Holy Spirit has placed a restriction on women taking the role of a teacher either over a group of men or a mixed group. In the Greek language, the word for teach is in a continual tense, i.e., "to continually teach." In other words, this Scripture is not forbidding women teaching, but rather forbidding having the office of a teacher over men. Kenneth Wuest, in his Greek commentary and expanded translation, brings this out: *I do not permit a woman to be a teacher [in an official position exercising authority over the man in church doctrine or discipline.]*[22]

The idea of a woman being quiet is also somewhat misleading. The same word in Greek is translated *quietness* (vs. 11) and *silence* (vs. 12). This word does not mean complete silence or not talking; it is also used in II Thes. 3:12, translated *to settle down* (NIV). Thayer's Greek Lexicon says it is used to describe the man or woman who does his own work and does not wrongly meddle in the affairs of others. In the Corinthian church Paul tells the women to be silent,[23] but in that context it seems that the women were interrupting, asking a lot of questions and causing disruption in the church.[24] Paul was not against women ever talking in church, because in the same book he also says they can pray and prophesy.[25]

The real issue in this passage is a woman wrongly exercising authority. The normal Greek word for *authority* (exousia) is not used here. Instead Paul uses a Greek word used only once in the New Testament, *authenteo*. One Greek dictionary says it is "one who acts on his own authority."[26] Therefore, this verse is speaking of a woman who authenticates herself; one who acts on her own authority, not God's. One interlinear translation gives a very plausible translation: *to exercise the authority of a man.*[27] The Greek does not include the word "over," which is used in some English translations. A woman, therefore, should not usurp authority which belongs to men.

In an assembly, it seems appropriate for a woman to pray, speak forth prophetically, testify of God's goodness, or even give a teaching on occasion. Paul did not entirely restrict women teaching. In his second letter to Timothy, Paul mentions the teaching influence of Timothy's godly mother and grandmother.[28] It is certainly proper for women to teach children in the home or Sunday school classes. It does seem improper, however, for women to take the role of a pastor or a regular teacher in a position over men. There is no record in the book of Acts of a woman publicly teaching or preaching over a group of men. It is a fundamental principle in God's dealings with mankind that men have been given the headship and women a place of submission.[29] Men and women are completely equal in their standing before God (Gal. 3:28). They are equal in essence, but different in function, just as are the three Persons of the Trinity. Women can certainly minister, but they are forbidden to be in a *functional* position of ecclesiastical authority over men, teaching them on a regular basis in a congregational setting.

What if a Woman is Already a Pastor of a Congregation?

While working with Christian leaders in Africa I have found a common dilemma: a woman becomes converted to Christ, goes back to her village, shares the good news, soon other people come to Christ, and suddenly she has a church of a few dozen people! So, what should this woman do?! In some cases, she has no spiritual men in the church. What is the solution to the dilemma?

First of all, we realize the Lord's church is in a state of growth and development; we *are being built together to become a dwelling in which God lives by his Spirit.*[30] No church has everything functioning perfectly according to the New Testament pattern. While God has a pattern for his church, he also has the sovereign right to make exceptions (which are consistent with his holy standards).

In such cases, where a woman has started a church in her village, it would be unhealthy for her to stop shepherding the flock. She should be faithful in her task of feeding the flock, who are looking to her for instruction and guidance. A spiritual mother should not abandon her children.

However, as the church becomes established, she should ask God to raise up male leaders.[31] She should seek after God's design for church government. As men arise, they should be given responsibility little by little. As they prove themselves faithful, more responsibilities can be given (Lk. 16:10). They can slowly emerge more publicly as leaders, and the woman can take a step backward. A team ministry can develop. The woman might remain in leadership, especially in an advisory capacity. The long-term goal will be more men actively leading. Most women pastors I have met would gladly welcome the assistance of godly male leaders.

What if We Have Been too Hasty and Picked Wrong Men for Elders?

This can indeed present a very serious problem and if not dealt with carefully, can wreak great havoc in a local congregation. We will need much wisdom from heaven to deal with this problem.

There are some men we should NOT appoint as elders:

- New converts. (I Tim. 3:6)
- Polygamists. (I Tim. 3:2)
- Ambitious men who enjoy the "limelight." (III John 9)
- Men who give a lot of money to the church, but lack in Christian character. (James 2:1-4)
- Men who are gifted as preachers but do not necessarily have a shepherd's heart for the people.

If we have been too hasty and picked the wrong men as elders, I recommend the following steps. First, we ought to get on our faces and confess our sin before God. If we too-hastily picked wrong men, it was a serious mistake. Let us pray and fast before taking any action. We must especially pray for minimum damage within the body.

After prayer, we should go to the brother one-on-one and honestly confront the issues about which we are concerned (Matt. 18:15). It may be possible for him to make adjustments and become a better leader.[32] If he resists correction, he must be asked to step down. This will take courage on our part.

If he does not want to step down, we could call in an apostle (a spiritual father you respect and if possible, a man who knows the other party) to talk to him (Matt. 18:16). If he still resists voluntarily stepping down, then a public meeting must be held and an announcement given about the removal of this man. This is a difficult process, but sometimes necessary for the preservation of the church. Even if there is a church split in this situation, it will ultimately be for good if it is done in the right way.

In summary, if we see the need for adding men as elders and the biblical mandate to *appoint elders in every town*, then we must realize in the initial stages of a new work, we may have to be the sole leader. But pray earnestly for God to raise up at least two other male leaders. Work with one, two, or three men who have leadership potential. Make room for other leaders. Seek to defer to faithful, younger men as they desire to serve Christ. As God raises up other capable leaders, it will be a good thing not only for us personally, but for the entire body.

Chapter Seven
Myths of the Ministry

Sam Puckett, 28 years old, finds himself at a crossroad.

For seven years Sam built a thriving men's clothing store business containing all the components for future financial success and security. However, two years ago things began to change. In an evangelistic meeting, Sam had heard the gospel message, surrendered his life to the Lordship of Jesus, and became a "new creature in Christ." Leaving a traditional church, he joined a local Bible church, an independent Bible-believing congregation. The pastor, excited about Sam's involvement in the church, following his conversion, is now urging Sam to "go into the ministry," preparing himself by attending Word Bible School. The pastor attended this school and it was instrumental in his own ordination into the ministry. Sam, who is growing dissatisfied with his secular work, is thinking he needs a drastic change in his life to "really serve Christ." Such a decision is not easy; it will involve his wife and two small children, his present business obligations and debts, and moving or commuting ninety miles to the school. Sam is at a crossroad and his dilemma is heightened by three common "myths of the ministry."

One definition of *myth* is "a widely held story or belief; a misconception; a misrepresentation of the truth."[1] Some great myths or misconceptions in Christendom involve our thinking about "the ministry." When a young man like Sam Puckett desires to serve God, the logical course to follow seems to be to "go into the ministry." There is much about this thinking that is detrimental to the body of Christ, and needs to be challenged by the word of God. This chapter will examine three common myths of the ministry. If some statements seem to be offensive or radical, I ask you simply to pray and consider the scriptural precedent, though it may "upset the apple cart." Let us pray that everything we read, including this chapter, will be sifted by the Holy Spirit, who has promised to lead us into all truth.

MYTH #1

"The Ministry" Is a Special Call For a Few Professionals

A fundamental truth of the New Testament is that ministry is not a function relegated to a select group of pastors, missionaries, and other "called" folks; we are all ministers.

> *Not that we are competent to claim anything for ourselves, but our competence comes from God. He has made us competent as ministers of a new covenant – not of the letter but of the Spirit . . .*[2]

Ministry is not for just a few "qualified" people; nor is it just for those in "gospel work;" it is for all of us. All believers are "ministers" in the Biblical sense of the word. Notice in the following verse that it is the *saints* who are to do the work of ministry: *His intention was the perfecting and the full equipping of the saints (His consecrated people), that they should do the work of ministering toward building up Christ's body (the church) . . .*[3]

There is no Biblical basis for limiting the name "minister" only to pastors and other church workers. The Greek word (diakonos) simply means a servant, often used for a willing servant.[4] In classical Greek it was sometimes used for "a waiter of

74

tables."[5] In modern language, such a person would be an "errand boy." The word "minister" is not a special ecclesiastical title for someone who is overly-zealous or does jobs we lesser mortals cannot do. When we say "Reverend Smith is the minister of our church," it implies (1) the church only has one minister; one man is essentially responsible for the work and (2) the rest of us are something other than ministers; we are an audience, spectators, or at best supporters, making sure our paid performer does his job correctly.

In many churches today we see a clergy/laity distinction which contributes much to a faulty concept of ministry. Our modern usage of the word "clergy" can be traced back to the Latin *clericatus*, which simply means "office of a priest."[6] Beginning in the second century, the scriptural concept that every believer is a priest[7] was gradually lost, and soon a select body of "qualified ministers" emerged who were expected to "keep things going." Their work soon became called "the ministry." Believers, therefore, began to look to a superstar leader, and Christianity became a spectator sport, like a typical pro-basketball game – ten men down on a court, desperately needing some rest, and ten thousand folks in the stands, desperately needing some exercise!

Clericalism is the expectation, both from the people and often from the pastor himself, that only professional clergy does the ministry; that any real ministry comes from an upper/middle class "polished personality." Paul Stevens explains further:

> "Clergy" is not so much a matter of position or being paid or having a title or receiving a certain status in the community. It is a whole mentality, a mentality of feeling responsible to provide the vision for the church, of leading the church, even running it. It is this feeling of indispensability that drives us to assume a responsibility for the church which rightfully belongs only to the Head, to Christ.[8]

Most evangelical churches in theory subscribe to the idea of "the priesthood of all believers," though they do not always put it into practice. Do qualified and gifted brothers, ordinary "laymen," ever speak on Sundays from the pulpit? Does the congregation become offended if the pastor shares the pulpit with members rather than guest speakers from elsewhere? Do members come with any anticipation and preparation to contribute to the meeting (e.g., a testimony, a song, a scripture, or a teaching[9])? Is there freedom for such body-ministry to occur under the direction of the Holy Spirit and wise leadership? Some reserved souls will be quick to quote the verse which says, *But everything should be done in a fitting and orderly way.*[10] They emphasize the latter part, *in a fitting and orderly way,* while they forget to follow the first part: *but everything should be done!*

Do many pastors allow marriage counseling by a non-professional couple who love the Lord, know the word, and demonstrate Christ's love by example in their home? The use of paid staff psychologist-counselors has become a commonly accepted practice and is widespread among evangelical churches. As a result, many Christians will only receive counseling from those whose profession it is. This is not to demean such counselors, but church members who know the New Testament teaching that we, as members of a body, are *competent to counsel one another,*[11] may receive effective ministry from other believers.

In our own local church, Sunday morning preaching/teaching is shared among five pastors and other capable brethren. When prayer requests are mentioned, a "pastoral prayer" is not necessary; concerned believers are encouraged to gather around the person in need, lay hands upon him, and pray the prayer of faith. Someone recently visited our church a couple of Sundays, then did not return. When a friend asked him why he left, he answered, "I want to go a church where there is a real pastor." In his mind, "pastor" was a full-time professional who had exclusive rights to pulpit ministry.

William Barclay, though a member of the very formal and liturgical Church of Scotland, was honest when he wrote,

Clearly the early Church had no professional ministry. . . . There is the obvious danger that when a man becomes a professional preacher he may sometimes be in the position of having to say something when he really has nothing to say. . . . It is a mistake to think that only the professional ministry can ever bring God's truth to man.[12]

Someone has said that perhaps we should dispense with the terms "clergy" and "laity" and invent a new term, "clayity," for we are all made of the same clay!

It is no easy matter to come into a proper concept of ministry. One step is the less frequent use of nametags. The disciples of Jesus would have been amazed (or amused) by the way we use nametags in our churches. The word "reverend" is enjoyed by many, yet it is used only once in the King James Bible and that is in reference to God: *Holy and reverend is his name.* (Ps. 111:9 KJV) We should be very hesitant to use any term which is used exclusively in describing God. The Revised Standard Version, instead of *reverend*, uses the word *terrible.* I wonder if those who like to be called "reverend" would also like to be called "terrible"?!

Notice how often these titles are used in the New Testament to describe Christians (NIV translation) :

- Pastor. 1
- Bishop....................... 0
- Clergyman 0
- Priest....................... 3
- Reverend 0
- Minister 6
- Servant 37
- Brother 187

Some leaders say it is good to use a title like "pastor" for respect. However, the Bible tells wives to *respect* their husbands,[13] but a respectful wife does not have to call her husband, "Husband John . . ." She can just call him, "John . . ."

So, if we are going to call ourselves by any name, maybe we should use the name *brother* a little more. Jesus said, *"But do not be called Rabbi; for one is your teacher, and you are all brothers."*[14] Alexander Strauch has observed,

It is deeply significant that the early Christians did not give lordly, hierarchical, or clerical titles to their leaders. Although both the Greeks and Jews had a wealth of titles for their political and religious leaders, the early Christians avoided borrowing such titles. Jesus explicitly forbids His followers from assuming honorific titles that separate and elevate one brother over another (Matthew 23:6-10). Therefore, the early Christians used lowly, unofficial, common, and functional words to describe themselves – brother, beloved, fellow-workers, laborers, slave, servant, prisoner, fellow-soldier, and steward. Even the leadership terms the New Testament writers used were generic terms that could easily be applied in the Christian context.

There were prophets, teachers, apostles, pastors, evangelists, leaders, elders, and deacons within the early church, but these terms were not used as formal titles. For example, all Christians are saints, but there is no "Saint John." All are priests, but there is no "Priest Philip." Some are elders, but there is no "Elder Paul." Some are pastors, but there is no "Pastor James." Some are deacons, but there is no "Deacon Andrew."

The array of ecclesiastical titles accompanying the names of Christian leaders today is completely missing from the New Testament, and would have appalled the apostles and early believers.[15]

MYTH #2

"The Ministry" Involves a Full Time Career in Gospel Work

In our opening narrative, Sam Puckett feels he needs to leave his secular job so he can "really serve Christ." This thinking reveals a common tradition that has paralyzed countless Christians. Many of us share the false assumption that unless we are working in a full-time gospel-oriented work, we are "second-class Christians" and are falling short of God's best for our lives.

In his excellent book, *Secular Work is Full-time Service*, Larry Peabody provides a proper perspective of serving the Lord:

> The New Testament draws no sacred/secular lines between Christians in "full-time service" and those in other types of work. In fact, the Bible does not contain the phrase "full-time Christian service." It teaches that all Christians should serve God full time, even though our differing vocations display such service in a variety of forms.
>
> It is true that some Christians are "set apart" for the gospel (Romans 1:1; Acts 13:2). But this setting apart does not mean total abstinence from ordinary work. Paul was set apart for gospel service, yet he frequently supported himself by working at a trade . . .
>
> In Scripture God has revealed to us the meaning of work. All work has meaning, whether it be scrubbing a floor or managing a corporation. . . . It is unthinkable that God's people should view ordinary work as second-best, as less significant than gospel work.[16]

We see no pattern in Scripture in which a believer received a sudden call, went through four to seven years of Bible school and seminary, and then entered a career of full-time gospel work. God seems to test his servants in the small, ordinary affairs of life before He entrusts spiritual responsibilities to them.[17] As it has been said, "You don't just go into the ministry; you *grow* into the ministry." The men God used in great ways were men who were first active and industrious in ordinary jobs:

- Elisha was plowing in a field when Elijah invited him.[18]
- Gideon was working in a wine press when God called him.[19]
- Moses was looking after sheep when the angel appeared.[20]
- David was keeping sheep when Samuel called.[21]

Many young pastors would be better equipped to deal with working people (the majority in most congregations) if they first engaged in secular work themselves. Paul Stevens, after pastoring 25 years, felt this lack in his own life, so for several years he took a part-time job as a carpenter as well as continuing his responsibilities in shepherding his flock. Coming to elders' meetings in blue jeans with a lunch box raised eyebrows. Once a board member inquired, "What's a pastor doing hammering nails?" It was a hard five years for Paul but it gave him greater identification with his members as well as encouraged the corporate body to share in ministry with him.[22]

I know a man who is very gifted in pastoring and teaching the word. After many years in several churches, faithfully serving the Lord, this brother feels that God wants him to be involved in a secular job and not in specific full-time gospel work. Many of his friends, especially other pastors, do not understand. They think he is "missing his call" and settling for something second-best.

Young Christian workers, by skipping secular work, may have missed out on one of the Lord's greatest training tools. Larry Peabody explains:

Our daily work serves as one of God's major tools for cultivating and nurturing the life of Christ within us. While we may be eager to have our work used in changing the lives of others, God is eager first to change our own lives through our work. . . . Through our work God brings into our lives circumstances which force us to choose between life and death to this self life. . . . Our work can, if we allow it and recognize God's hand in it, be used to grind us, smooth us, polish us, and fit us for the service of the living God.[23]

Derek Prince, a former Cambridge professor and international Bible teacher for more than forty years, contributed this testimony:

People ask me where I received my training for the ministry. Sometimes I answer, "As a medical orderly with the British Army in North Africa." I had had academic training before I knew the Lord. In fact, I was over-balanced intellectually. What I needed was experience in confronting tough, real life situations and accepting responsibility for the needs of others.[24]

Is it a coincidence that the greatest minister of all time had a public ministry of only three years and yet was "confined" in the limitations of home life and a secular job as a carpenter for thirty years prior to his public ministry? Did Jesus feel he was falling short or just "passing time" as he faithfully hammered nails in an obscure village? Although there is nothing magical about the number thirty, the number is seen several other times in regard to ministry:

• David was thirty when God finally established his kingship. (First he had to endure many years fleeing from Saul and living in caves).[25]

• Joseph was thirty when he entered the service of Pharaoh, king of Egypt. (First he had to work as a servant to Potiphar and live in a prison).[26]

81

- Young men had to be at least thirty to serve in the tabernacle.[27]

- Some men with major ministries in recent times, such as Bill Bright and Bill Gothard, were first faithful in ordinary work until they were thirty. This is also true of lesser men of God, not as well known, like myself! After graduating from a Christian university with a Bible degree, I worked in a family retail furniture business for seven years. At age thirty-two I was ordained an elder and began working full-time in our church and school ministry.

This is not to limit the Holy Spirit from using younger men. Indeed, Church history is full of examples of young men who were mightily used of God.[28] The point here is that God uses as many or even more people who have been trained by the "school of life" as he does those trained in academic institutions, and much of this training occurs in secular jobs. I have met young men who were eager to be evangelists or pastors, and yet they had never learned to hold down a secular job for any length of time, to be respectful to employers, to get along with fellow-employees, and to work hard "as unto the Lord." Judson Cornwall gave some good advice to a graduating class at a Bible college in the East:

Now that you have learned everything this erudite faculty has been able to teach you, for God's sake, for the Church's sake, and for your own sake, do not immediately enter full-time Christian service. Most of you came directly from high school to this Bible school, and you have not learned how to live responsibly in this world. Go out and get jobs. Learn how to handle money and how to relate to people outside your religious walls. Then, when you have matured as people, let God call you into leadership in His Church.[29]

The idea of secular work should never be dismissed by the Christian worker. One person who embodies this truth is the apostle Paul. Paul taught that a salary was sometimes appropriate for a worker in the gospel.[30] Although he received financial gifts at times,[31] he said, *"I have never taken advantage of any such right."*[32] Paul often provided for himself and others by making tents.[33] He warned against laziness and endorsed the work ethic:

> *For you yourselves know how you ought to follow our example. We were not idle when we were with you, nor did we eat anyone's food without paying for it. On the contrary, we worked night and day, laboring and toiling so that we would not be a burden to any of you. We did this, not because we do not have the right to such help, but in order to make ourselves a model for you to follow.*[34]

Paul was flexible. He was available to preach the gospel as the Lord directed, but he was also prepared to work with his hands when the need arose. He had no security or pension plan from gospel work.

A pastor I once met was struggling in a small church with little responsibility and little income. My suggestion was: "Why not get a part-time secular job to supplement your income?" His reaction was such that he hardly entertained my suggestion as a possibility. He apparently has believed a myth of ministry.

MYTH #3
We are Best Trained for the Ministry Through Bible School or Seminary

In the introduction, both Sam Puckett and his pastor are convinced the answer for Sam's burning desire to serve the Lord is to be found by going off to Bible school. Most churches today require formal theological training before allowing someone to speak on a regular basis from the pulpit or to be recognized as a shepherd of God's flock. Does this thinking have a Biblical basis, or is it one more "myth of the ministry?"

Let us notice first of all the Biblical requirements for a church leader (pastor/elder):

I TIMOTHY 3:2-7	TITUS 1:6-9
1. Above reproach	1. Blameless
2. Husband of one wife	2. Husband of one wife
3. Temperate who believe	3. Having children
4. Self-controlled	4. Not overbearing
5. Respectable	5. Not quick-tempered
6. Hospitable wine	6. Not given to much
7. Able to teach	7. Not violent
8. Not given to much wine	8. Not pursuing dishonest gain
9. Not violent	9. Hospitable
10. Gentle	10. Loves what is good
11. Not quarrelsome	11. Self-controlled
12. Not a lover of money	12. Upright
13. Manages family well	13. Holy
14. Not a recent convert	14. Disciplined
15. A good reputation with those outside the church	15. Holding fast the message; able to refute those who contradict it

In all of these qualities, we see that the chief emphasis is on *character*, not academics. Only those men who are *spiritually* and *morally* qualified should be leaders in the Lord's church. Of all the qualities, only one in each listing is related to academics ("able to teach" and "able to . . . refute those who contradict it").

In his excellent book, *Biblical Eldership*, Alexander Strauch points out two extremes regarding the qualifications of church leaders. First, we sometimes ignore the full range of scriptural qualifications above, thus permitting unqualified men to fill a crucial position of leadership. The second extreme is to add qualifications that God does not demand, thus excluding needed and qualified men from church leadership.[35]

In many churches gifted and qualified saints sit idle, unable to minister in a public meeting because they are not "properly qualified." Roland Allen (1868-1947), an Anglican missiologist, wrote about this subject (his reference to the "apostolic" referred to the apostle Paul's qualifications listed above):

> We are so enamored of those qualifications which we have added to the apostolic that we deny the qualifications of anyone who possesses only the apostolic, whilst we think a man qualified who possesses only ours. A young student fresh from a theological college lacks many of those qualifications which the apostle deemed necessary for a leader in the house of God, the age, the experience, the established position and reputation, even if he possesses all the others. Him we do not think unqualified. The man who possesses all the apostolic qualifications is said to be unqualified, because he cannot go back to school and pass an examination.[36]

Academics and good theological training can certainly be of value to anyone desiring to serve Christ, if they are put in proper priority. Our seminaries and Bible schools should never be belittled, as they have a history in our nation of contributing to the lives of countless saints and providing a bulwark against false doctrines and movements. However, no matter how good it is, education will not complete the training of a man. Charles Jefferson, in *The Minister as Shepherd*, observed, "The minister has become too much a man of a book. Like the ancient scribes, he is a scholar and sometimes a pedant.[37] (A "pedant" is a person who makes an excessive display of his learning.)

I recently read the requirements for ministry and ordination in three of our well-known theological seminaries: Yale, Princeton, and Harvard. The emphasis for graduation includes:

- Knowledge of Greek, Hebrew, German, or Latin
- Understanding of different religions
- Familiarity with church polity and procedures
- Writing an acceptable thesis
- Studies in philosophy, psychology, and sociology

While none of these studies are bad in themselves, they may not be adequate for properly training the man of God. There was little mention in these seminary requirements about maturity of character or practical, proven ministry experience. I once talked with a seminary professor who expressed a dilemma: "What do we do with a young man who has all the academic qualifications to begin ministry in a church, but character-wise he is not mature enough? How can we send him out with our blessing?"

One of the main problems with an over-emphasis on academic qualifications is that it severely limits ministry. Not only are gifted people kept from public ministry, but a highly-educated minister will often have a limited audience. Donald McGavran, a professor at Fuller Theological Seminary and recognized leader in church research, stated:

Be assured that I am not advocating scant training for ministers . . . It does need to be said, however, that there is a danger that highly educated men will not be heard by large segments of the population . . . they will remain out of touch with blue-collar America and some of white-collar America also.[38]

In his research McGavran points out that the fastest growing denominations in our country's history were those that frequently used Spirit-filled men who had relatively little formal education.[39] Many of those most effective in advancing God's kingdom have been men without formal theological education: such notables as John Bunyan, C. H. Spurgeon, D. L. Moody, G. Campbell Morgan, A. W. Tozer, and Billy Graham, to name a few.

So far we have examined three great myths of "the ministry." However, lest our focus center just on where we have fallen short, we must also consider some alternate possibilities. In the next chapter, we will further explore ideas of training for ministry.

Chapter Eight
God's Training Program For His Servants

In the last chapter we examined three common myths of the ministry, including our current methods of training Christian workers. As we have stated, to send off a young family man to a three or four year theological institute will usually be hard on his married life, be quite expensive, often require irrelevant classes, and be completely disconnected from his local church. Are we missing something? Is there a better way? What is the biblical concept of training for greater service in the body of Christ?

1. We are trained as we grow in our personal knowledge of Christ.

The best that we contribute to others is that which we have experienced as part of our lives. Our relationship with Christ is one in which *in Him we live and move and have our being.*[1] When Paul ministered to the Thessalonian church he shared with them not only the gospel truth, but his own life as well. The men I have admired most have been those who have not gained knowledge about Christ merely from a textbook, but those "seasoned saints" who, over many years, have learned a personal, intimate knowledge of Christ reflected in their actions and attitudes. These men and women have learned much through weathering life's storms and glorifying God in all circumstances.

Robert Murray McCheyne received his training this way; he was educated at Edinburgh University over a century ago. McCheyne became a Christian at age 18 and was later ordained a pastor in the Church of Scotland. This man was used as an instrument of great revival in Scotland in his day. His preparation for ministry, however, came from walking with Christ through some tough times. His biographer described his experience:

> His soul was prepared for the awful work of ministry by much prayer, and much study of the word of God; by affliction in his person; by inward trials and sore temptations; by experience of the depth of corruption in his own heart, and by discoveries of the Saviour's fulness of grace.[2]

McCheyne's belief was "to be in Christ before being in the ministry."[3] To him, it was an indispensable tenet.

2. We are trained as we become disciplined by the Holy Spirit.

We live in an "instant-society" where life is fast-paced and most desires can be obtained fairly quickly. This is not so in becoming a useful vessel in God's kingdom.

God's training is "on-the-job" training; we "grow as we go." It is not usually accomplished through four to seven years of classroom study. Moses, who was *educated in all the wisdom of the Egyptians,*[4] still needed forty years of character training in the wilderness. In his booklet, *Your Training or You?*, G. M. Cowan shared his concern:

> Perhaps a large part of our trouble is that we tend to think of "training" as something of itself, a period of time, certain courses taken, a degree earned, abilities and qualifications that can be listed and enumerated on paper, so many credit hours, rather than as *something that has happened to us . . .*

Of itself training is nothing. *It is the trained man that God uses.* And God's training may include both formal and informal education.[5]

One thing is certain – if we have been truly trained under the leadership of the Holy Spirit and not just the textbook, every aspect of our character will be refined and brought under the lordship of Christ to serve his ends. DeVern Fromke emphasized the goal of any training:

Essential training, then, should produce disciplined – self-disciplined, Spirit-disciplined men – who know how to exercise wise control over their time, appetites, passions, tongue, thoughts; men who have learned how to operate on a Spirit-directed system of priorities, on their own, away from the helpful stimulus of Christian fellowship and meetings, or in the midst of pressure toward mediocrity among many Christians. We can see why so much training has failed; it is not mere skills and knowledge attained but the *character produced* that is basic to the resilience and flexibility necessary to meet situations without cracking.[6]

Modern training is primarily intellectual; New Testament training is primarily spiritual and practical. Modern training emphasizes the classroom; New Testament training also emphasizes life and experience. Modern training targets young men and women; New Testament training includes older saints as well. Modern training occurs at schools or programs often hundreds of miles away from one's home; New Testament training can occur in one's local church and community.

In the apostle Paul's "training" for ministry, God used many circumstances in molding this former persecutor into a "vessel of honor." Paul had been highly educated under the renowned

Gamaliel in his pre-Christian days. God, however, chose other means in training his servant. After Paul's conversion, he immediately began preaching Christ, but in Damascus, he was threatened with death and had to take a humble exit, being lowered in a basket from the city wall.[7] Paul later mentioned this experience as one of the events that qualified him to be a servant of God.[8] In another place, he gives a list of other experiences which contributed to his formation as a genuine minister of God: *We give no offense in anything, that our ministry may not be blamed. But in all things we commend ourselves as ministers of God: in much patience, in tribulations, in needs, in distresses . . .*[9]

How many of us would sign up for Paul's "seminary"?!

3. We are trained through short-term seminars and regular, disciplined reading of good books.

We often see truth through our American eyeglasses. Some of our concepts of training are not very applicable in most of the world. A few years ago there was a meeting of Trainers of Pastors International Consultation (TOPIC), sponsored by the Billy Graham Center at Wheaton. Representatives attended from over a hundred organizations involved in training pastors in Second and Third World countries. In this meeting, several facts were brought forth:

- Of two million pastoral leaders currently serving congregations, only 5% (100,000) have had formal training.
- It is not appropriate to move most of them from homes, churches and jobs to spend long periods of time in formal academic settings (Bible schools, seminaries, etc.)
- The most appropriate training is frequent short-term seminars supplemented by good literature.[10]

I can confirm this truth as I have had the privilege over the past ten years of conducting Leaders Seminars in Uganda and India. As I have met with hundreds of pastors and church leaders

I have realized much of our American Bible school curriculum would be overwhelming and irrelevant. I have worked closely with local leaders to determine what subjects are pertinent and developed a seminar book of notes for those who can read English. We meet for about four full days and cover most of the book. For the majority of leaders with whom we have met, it is the only teaching seminar they have ever attended. We also try to get some good, basic teaching books and Bible dictionaries in their hands. Our method may seem simple, but it has had much good fruit wherever we have gone and seems to lay a good foundation.

I have seen another good model for Bible training in a program conducted by Alex Mitala and other leaders in Uganda. Alex, currently the "General Overseer" of the National Fellowship of the Born Again Fellowships in Uganda, leads a one-month Bible training program which is very practical for young, married pastors. These pastors leave their families during the weekdays for four weeks, live in dormitories, and study the word of God all day long. There is a modest fee for the school with some scholarships available. Taught by four teachers, the pastors get an excellent Bible education over the month, and they are given a certificate in a ceremony upon completion. This way, they are not gone for long periods from their family or church. A second and third level of study is also available if they want to return at some future time. This type of program is so much more accessible than a three or four year program Westerners deem so important.

Any of us can also learn a lot from regular, disciplined reading. In my own life, I benefitted from majoring in Bible at a Christian University. However, my best professors directed me to read good books. Over my thirty five years as a Christian I have gained a valuable (and hopefully balanced) education through an ongoing, disciplined reading of good Christian books. Godly men can recommend books to you, and I can suggest a good starter list in my notes.[11]

4. We are trained in our local church.

At twenty years of age I left home and traveled a thousand miles to attend a Christian university. The many Bible classes I took were interesting and some extremely valuable in my life, and relationships with professors were precious. However, my greatest learning during those years came about from my involvement in a large, vibrant church family which tried to follow New Testament patterns. Through sound and practical Bible teaching, personal discipleship programs, accountability for godly behavior, and the care of leaders, my life was greatly affected for good. A friend and I approached one of the pastors and asked him to spend time with us, sharing his life and the "nuts and bolts" of his effective ministry. This pastor, already extremely busy, undertook the additional responsibility. He took a personal interest in these two young college students, meeting with us weekly, hosting us in his home, and occasionally taking us with him when ministering in other cities. It was a most valuable education.

The local church should be thought of as "God's workshop;" it should be a training center that prepares for ministry.[12] Too often the local church has not even been considered as an instrument in training believers for ministry. Paul Stevens comments:

> The best structure for equipping every Christian is already in place. It predates the seminary and the weekend seminar and will outlast both. In the New Testament no other nurturing and equipping agency is offered than the local church. In the New Testament church, as in the ministry of Jesus, people learned in the furnace of life, in a relational, living, working and ministering context.[13]

Alexander Hay, General Superintendent of New Testament Missionary Union, cautioned about separating theological training from the local church.

94

To separate those who are to be trained for ministry from normal church life and activity and from the conditions in which their ministry is to be carried on is a serious mistake. One preparing for the ministry of evangelism and church planting needs the church and the evangelistic field just as the medical student needs the hospital and the clinic. To send out a young man to practice medicine who had little more than theoretical knowledge, who had little practical experience and never even seen a major operation performed, would not be justifiable. It would be hard on both the young physician and his patients![14]

More academic training may be necessary for some believers. Some believers will feel called to specialized ministries, which most local churches may not be able to provide training for. Others may feel called to work in academic circles. One will need at least a Master's degree to have an open door of ministry in many educational institutions. But, for most believers, the local church ought to provide adequate training.

Some might respond by asking, "What if there is nobody in my local church who can help equip me?" My response is that possibly such a one is in the wrong church. God's church was never intended to be a static thing; if we can neither contribute or receive ministry in a given church, we would be better off elsewhere. T. A. Sparks emphasized the vital importance of the local church:

The training of workers should be in close relationship with church life as constituted and formed on the true organic basis of the body of Christ. Not just a preaching place, or one where meetings are held and attended; but where there is true corporate life and building up. In such, and out from such corporate life, ministry and service should be developed; not just technicians from an institute. No one should really be allowed to go into whole time Christian service who has not had a true "church" training and learned the meaning and value of corporate life.[15]

Seminaries, Bible schools, and para-church discipleship programs can certainly contribute to equipping saints. But, why have we neglected the local church as the place of preparation? Why is it that in the majority of churches, leaders have to be chosen from outside the church body? Why is it, that when some pastors travel, they invite an outside speaker to come in? Is there no man among the congregation who is an example of Christ and has the word of Christ dwelling within? If so, then equipping has not been taking place, and the church is being trained to be "spoon-fed" by the "professional." The New Testament pattern was not to send away for substitutes; rather, local leadership was raised up from within the body.[16] These local leaders, for the most part, probably did not leave their normal occupations. They were men who had grown up within a congregation, who had shown themselves faithful in smaller tasks, who met the qualifications of I Timothy 3, and in the Lord's proper timing were publicly recognized (ordained) as men who were shepherds after God's heart.

5. We are trained through small groups or one-on-one mentoring relationships.

How did Jesus, the Master Teacher do it? Did he enroll all the disciples in a Wednesday night class? Did he send them off to a Jerusalem theological school? Notice Jesus' original call to his disciples. *He appointed twelve–designating them apostles–that they might be with him and that he might send them out to preach and to have authority to drive out demons.*[17]

Jesus seemed to have little interest in relationships which were merely technical or informational. He chose the twelve disciples first and foremost to *be with him*; then out of a

96

relationship came ministry. Jesus spent a major amount of his time with twelve men, three of whom he was especially close to. His training was "on-the-job training," not a formal series of Bible studies. In the first year with Jesus, it seems the disciples were basically observing and listening to Jesus. In Jesus' third tour of Galilee, later in their second year together, the disciples were sent out in pairs on short trips.[18] After they returned, Jesus gave them further instruction and correction. Robert Coleman, in his classic *Master Plan of Evangelism*, describes Jesus' method of training:

> When one stops to think of it, this was an incredibly simple way of doing it. Jesus had no formal school, no seminaries, no outlined course of study, no periodic membership classes in which he enrolled His followers. None of these highly organized procedures considered so necessary today entered at all into His ministry. Amazing as it may seem, all Jesus did to teach these men His way was to draw them close to Himself. He was His own school and curriculum.[19]

This is not to demean the value of systematic Bible study. The format of study, however, should always be secondary to the relationship between the teacher and those who are being taught. Jesus said, *A pupil is not above his teacher; but everyone, after he has been fully trained, will be like his teacher.*[20] Notice Jesus did not say, "*think* like his teacher . . ." but "*be* like his teacher." Effective teaching is personal, and if so, it will naturally duplicate something of the teacher into the students' lives.

Paul's method of training was also very personal. He told Timothy, *The things which you have heard from me in the presence of many witnesses, entrust these to faithful men who will be able to teach others also.*[21] Paul taught Timothy and he expected him in return to teach faithful men who in turn would teach others. This was how leadership was developed. Probably most New

Testament training took place in informal settings with small groups or one-on-one relationships. When Paul traveled on his missionary journeys, he sometimes took a group of younger men with him.[22]

Much can be imparted through the relationship of an older, seasoned saint and a younger brother who is zealous for the ways of the Lord. The relationship may be an ongoing friendship, or it may be short-term. A few years after Paul became converted, he visited Peter for fifteen days: *Then after three years, I went up to Jerusalem to get acquainted with Peter and stayed with him fifteen days.*[23] This was more than just a casual acquaintance; the Greek language here implies "a visit for the purpose of coming to know someone."[24] Peter did not enroll Paul in a systematic three-year Bible study to make sure he had all his doctrine straight; most likely they enjoyed intimate fellowship together, and Peter related to Paul much of his first-hand knowledge of the life, ministry, and teaching of our Lord.

Sometimes God uses longer relationships to develop a man or woman of God. Joshua as a younger man (in his forties) was a helper to Moses; he was Moses' right-hand-man. Later he succeeded Moses in leading Israel. Elisha also spent time with an older man; for possibly several years he "tagged along" with Elijah and was his "errand boy," before stepping into his own ministry. Paul discipled Timothy, but it was his ongoing, godly example – as much as his teaching – that influenced Timothy:

> But you, Timothy, have known intimately both what I have taught and how I have lived. My purpose and my faith are no secrets to you. You saw my endurance and love and patience as I met all those persecutions and difficulties . . .[25]

These kind of "apprentice" or "mentoring" relationships may do more to train men than any course of study.

It is imperative that we carefully consider how we train future Christian workers both here and abroad. Ralph Winter, director of the U. S. Center for World Mission, issued this caution.

> Despite the perspective of missionaries sent out from the United States, the Christian movement on a global level continues doggedly to depend on informal apprenticeship methods of ministerial training rather than the historically recent European style of professional education in residential schools. This is mainly because apprenticeship is more versatile and flexible than the classroom. . . . The fact is that wherever seminaries or other types of lengthy residential programs have been introduced overseas *and made mandatory for ordination,* the growth of the church has been severely crippled.[26]

Both formal and informal means may be used in the training of leaders. Whatever methods are used, however, the local church, "God's workshop," should not be secondary in developing His people for service. Any training method will also be most effective if it is personal between the instructor and student. Under the discipline of the Holy Spirit we can be prepared adequately for effective works of service.

SECTION THREE

THE FUNCTIONING CHURCH

Chapter Nine
The Church in the Home

For the first ten years of our church's history, we met in a home. We first met in a living room, then moved into a bigger dining area, and finally into a large auxiliary meeting room. When we outgrew the home, we began to think about purchasing a building we could use for church meetings. Our years in that modest home have left some very special memories and laid a foundation of relational Christianity which has remained with us to this day.

We now own a building which is jointly used by a Christian high school and our church. We have a sign at our entry way which says . . .

> *The Meeting Place of*
> *Community Fellowship*
> *Church*

This sign is no small statement as to our emphasis and, occasionally, we remind the congregation what it is saying. One Sunday morning I asked our congregation, "How many of you believe this meeting room is a sanctuary?" Some hands rose reservedly as they were expecting a "trick" question. Then I explained, "A sanctuary is a 'holy place.' Is this meeting room a holy place? In one sense we could say it is 'set apart' for God's purposes. Yet, if I am having a fellowship gathering in my home, is it equally a 'holy place?' When I meet for an early morning study with some men at McDonald's restaurant, is it any less a 'holy place?' In the Old Covenant we see a building set aside as a holy temple, but in the New Covenant, *we are the temple of the living God.*[1] In the New Covenant there is no emphasis on holy buildings, only holy people."

In Christendom today we emphasize church buildings a great deal and yet often neglect the primary meeting place in the early church – the home. Howard Snyder, in his excellent book – *The Problem of Wineskins*, has addressed this issue well.

"If you had asked, 'Where is the church?' in any important city of the ancient world where Christianity had penetrated in the first century, you would have been directed to a group of worshiping people gathered in a house. There was no special building or other tangible wealth with which to associate 'church,' only people," so wrote the late Walter Oetting in a significant little book, *The Church of the Catacombs.*

Christians did not begin to build church buildings until about 200 A.D. This fact suggests that, whatever else church buildings are good for, they are not essential either for numerical growth or spiritual depth. The early church possessed both these qualities, and the church's greatest period of vitality and growth until recent times was during the first two centuries A.D. In other words, the church grew fastest when it did not have the help – or hindrance – of church buildings.[2]

Church buildings are sometimes necessary – especially for larger congregations, but the primary life of the church should be more centered in our homes. Notice in the book of Acts how homes were used in the life of the church:

- Seeking the Lord (2:2)
- Eating meals together/sharing communion (2:46)
- Planned meeting to hear the gospel (10:22)
- Prayer meeting (12:12)
- Impromptu evangelistic meeting (16:32)
- Discussing the word of God with a confused man (18:26)
- Whole night of fellowship and instruction (20:7)
- Teaching (20:20)
- Evening of fellowship (21:8)
- Talking with inquirers about the kingdom (28:30-31)

Mere Meetings or More Personal Fellowship?

God, who has called you into fellowship with his Son Jesus Christ our Lord, is faithful.[3]

God's call on our lives is first and foremost a call into vital relationship with Himself and other believers. The kind of fellowship pictured in the New Testament (the Greek word for fellowship is *koinonia*) was much more than Christians visiting or even attending Bible studies together; it involved an intimate sharing of a common life – life which was based on and centered in Jesus Christ. This was not something that happened in one or two meetings a week. It was a lifestyle:

They met constantly to hear the apostles teach, and to share the common life, to break bread, and to pray.[4]

What we have seen and heard we declare to you, so that you and we together may share a common life, that life which we share with the Father and his Son Jesus Christ.[5]

Dietrich Bonhoeffer, a pastor in the German church who resisted Hitler's Nazi movement, wrote an exceptional book about fellowship called *Life Together*.[6] This title aptly describes the relationships believers should enjoy. The early Christians met constantly – whether it was at the temple, the marketplace, or their homes. They enjoyed spending time daily with their Lord and with each other. Their fellowship was not limited to a Sunday morning gathering and possibly a Wednesday night meeting. Jerry Bridges, in his book, *True Fellowship*, wrote,

> Many Christians have recognized that there is a deeper and richer meaning to the Biblical concept of fellowship. They are not content with the idea of mere social activity. Among these people it is not unusual to hear someone say, "Let's get together for some fellowship." What these people usually mean is, "Let's get together to share with each other from the Bible and pray together." Or perhaps these people bring each other up to date on how God has been working in each of their lives. These certainly are important spiritual activities, and they are certainly a part of Biblical fellowship. Yet even these activities fail to capture the rich, full meaning of the fellowship described to us in the New Testament.[7]

There is a subtle danger that any assembly can fall into – holding the idea that fellowship only occurs in official meetings. One brother shared this exhortation:

> Meetings are not the pinnacle of Christian service. If we are not living it in our homes, with our families and roommates, and taking it to the streets and jobs . . . then our meetings, no matter how formal or how "free," will be a dangerous farce. The "excellent meetings" will be a very deceitful substitute for a corporate Christ-

life that truly celebrates Jesus together in Life, as well as in meetings. It's extremely misleading to say or act like "meetings" are what Christianity is all about (even when filled with lively praise). This is deceiving because it seems "so spiritual" to sing songs and to pray and to hear powerful teaching from the Word of God. However, a glimpse into the life of Jesus and the record of His church can only lead us to the conclusion that "spiritual meetings" are not the essence of Christianity.[8]

Our society is becoming more and more self-centered, with families isolating themselves in their own little worlds with their personal pursuits. Busyness is the sign of our times, and believers are often caught up in the "rat race" as much as the rest of the world – in a whirlwind of places to go, activities to do, and meetings to attend. Disregarding the word of the Lord, *Be still and know that I am God*,[9] it seems easy to fill our schedules with a multitude of personal plans that will have little value in eternity. This condition is aptly described by the prophet Haggai: *My house . . . remains a ruin, while each of you is busy with his own house.*[10] Wayne Jacobsen commented on the busyness syndrome:

> We've become a nation of activity junkies. Ask people how they are doing, and nine out of ten will find some way to let you know how busy they are. Though we complain about our busyness, we don't really hate it. If we did, we would stop . . . Busyness makes us feel important. Who has ever seen an "important" person who is not rushing off with something else to do?[11]

Some believers are so busy, they have no significant interaction with Christians other than one or two official meetings a week. This will greatly hinder the corporate life of that church. God has not called us to be a collection, but a community of saints who are actively involved in the lives of each other.

We must return to the home as the primary place of fellowship. It is sad to see a group of fifteen to twenty believers who have been gathered together by the Lord start talking about buying land and building a facility. Why not meet in homes until we are "bursting at the seams?" I have seen churches have prayer meetings and only ten believers gather in a building that will seat 300 people. Again, why not be more personal and meet in someone's home?

True fellowship can and should take place throughout the week in non-official meeting settings: talking about the Lord with fellow believers at work; taking initiative and visiting a shut-in or someone who is new in the assembly; and eating meals together. Some of my best fellowship has occurred at early morning breakfast get-togethers around a table at a local restaurant. Sometimes we study a Christian book, but the first half of our time is always spent in Christ-centered sharing of our lives with one another. Fellowship among us is always primary; any book study will be secondary. For fellowship to take place, it only takes two or three believers *gathered together in His name*[12] – and this can happen just about any place or any time during the week.

Practice Hospitality

Repeatedly we are encouraged by scripture to *practice hospitality*.[13] This means being willing to have people in our homes – even strangers.[14] There are probably many reasons we are negligent in this regard:

1. Our busy lifestyle ("We just don't have time for it.")
2. Self-centeredness ("I just stick to myself.")
3. Love of comfort ("I work hard and just like to relax when I get home . . .")
4. Insecurity ("We had a bad experience in the past.")
5. Pride ("My house isn't nice enough.")

6. Lack of initiative ("We tried that once but nobody ever invited us back!")

7. No interest in new people. ("We don't want to mess up our nice little group.")

8. Hypocrisy ("I do not really want people to come into my home and see how my family functions.")

One may think he is experiencing wonderful fellowship when he meets with a half a dozen people who are well-liked friends. There is nothing wrong with that, but is this what Christian community is all about – just meeting with people we know and like in the "inner circle?" There is a deeper level of koinonia fellowship.

> *When you give a luncheon or dinner, do not invite your friends, your brothers or relatives, or your rich neighbors; if you do, they may invite you back and so you will be repaid. But when you give a banquet, invite the poor, the crippled, the lame, the blind, and you will be blessed. Although they cannot repay you, you will be repaid at the resurrection of the righteous.*[15]

Hospitality is love in action. Peter in his first epistle encourages deep love: *Above all, love each other deeply, because love covers over a multitude of sins.*[16] The very next verse tells us how: *Offer hospitality to one another without grumbling.*[17] The J. B. Phillips translation gets more specific, *Be hospitable to each other without secretly wishing you hadn't got to be!*[18]

How do we view our home? Is it our home – or is it the Lord's home? We should see our homes we live in not as a possession we own but a gift God has given us to use in his kingdom. We should desire to bring church life into our homes in a greater measure. Scripture says, *Every day they continued to meet together in the temple courts. They broke bread in their homes and ate together with glad and sincere hearts.*[19]

Practical Suggestions

My wife and I both work outside the home and live full lives. At times we just have to sit down and plan out how we can interact more with people. Here a few ways we are still learning to be more hospitable.

1. Invite brethren over for an evening.

It does not have to be for a meal. Snacks or a dessert might be all that is needed. You can invite an entire family, a few couples, or a single person. Stop and consider the newer people in your church. Is there anybody who is unlikely to get invited by anyone else? Remember, it does not have to be a grand event; you can just visit or play a game together.

2. Be willing to host a home fellowship group.

For years my wife and I have had home groups meet during the mid-week which provide a smaller setting for Bible discussion, prayer, and sharing one another's burdens. Some have been very successful and some not. We usually take the initiative to invite certain folks, leaving the "door open" for others to attend as well.

Our home and yard do not have to be perfect. At our first home, we lived on the side of a hill with twenty-seven steps to the front door, no driveway, and little off-street parking. It did not hinder our hospitality.

3. Reach out to neighbors.

We invite people to church meeting; do we invite them to our home? Why not? Are we too dependent on a preacher to share Christ? Are we too insecure to reach out to new folks? In today's society, neighbors do not interact as they did many years ago. Sometimes we do not even know our neighbors by name.

Be creative. Occasionally my wife has baked a pie and taken it to a new neighbor. Once we invited our entire neighborhood over for Christmas refreshments. At times we have invited a next-door neighbor over for dessert and a game. Michael Green, an often quoted authority on evangelism, said, "One of the most effective methods of spreading the gospel in antiquity was by use of homes."[20] Robert and Julia Banks made a similar point, "It is often forgotten that the Christianity which conquered the Roman Empire was essentially a home centered movement."[21] We do not share Christ every time we get together with a neighbor, but spiritual conversations sometimes arise, or a neighbor will ask us to pray when facing a crisis. Two different neighbors – whom we knew little – asked me to do family funerals.

4. If you are a couple, work together.

It takes two to make hospitality work. If I was not willing to pitch in and help clean up the house or grill the chicken, my wife would not be as enthusiastic about hospitality. Sometimes men are not sensitive to this and the wife ends up visiting very little because she is doing all the work. Think these things over; talk to your mate and get a "game plan."

5. For those with hectic schedules, consider just once a month inviting over someone we do not know as well.

If every one of us in the local assembly took this simple action, it would help break up "cliques" or close-knit home groups in the church. It would also be a great blessing to the life of our church.

Let us not restrict our corporate Christian life to a meeting or two each week. Let us become more involved with one another. Let us be willing to take greater initiative in reaching out to others – especially new people with whom God seems to be connecting us.

Chapter Ten
The Role of the Holy Spirit in Corporate Meetings

Frank does not have a very good relationship with his wife, Sarah. He lives with her under the same roof, he makes constant use of her services, and he expects her to "be there" when he needs her. Frank, however, fails to communicate with Sarah, he seldom recognizes her presence, and he fails to enjoy her potential friendship. Frank's relationship with Sarah is lacking, to say the least, yet it is comparable to the relationship many believers have with the Holy Spirit.

Many of us agree in doctrine that the Holy Spirit is God and part of the Trinity. As far as knowing the person of the Holy Spirit and his working in practical ways is concerned, far too often our knowledge is limited. To some, the Holy Spirit is just a theological concept or an impersonal "force." For others, who believe in the Holy Spirit, *the fellowship of the Holy Spirit*[1] is often not a reality. Fellowship with the Holy Spirit means we personally commune with him. Instead of treating the Holy Spirit as a waiter in a restaurant, we need to invite his presence, his anointing, his leading, and his comfort. Whenever we read Scriptures we should invite the Holy Spirit to teach us; we should never assume that we will learn anything without his revelation to our hearts.[2]

In this chapter, we cannot present a comprehensive teaching about the Holy Spirit. There are important topics such as the baptism of the Holy Spirit, the fruit of the Holy Spirit, and walking in the Holy Spirit. Our focus, however, is simply on giving the Holy Spirit his rightful place as we meet corporately.

T. Austin-Sparks, a Bible teacher who had much insight into the body of Christ, was quite honest about a major weakness he saw among evangelical believers:

> The writer, over a period of nearly forty years of personal contact with evangelical Christianity in many parts of the world, has been terribly impressed with one basic weakness or defect. . . . While the doctrine of the Holy Spirit is well known . . . [we must ask] the question as to whether or not the majority of Christians know anything about the Holy Spirit as a positive, active, indwelling presence.[3]

The Holy Spirit as Initiator

The book of Acts is not to be thought of as merely the acts of the apostles; rather this book of early church history is the record of the acts *of the Holy Spirit* through the apostles. The Holy Spirit appears throughout this book, and we can quickly conclude that he, and not man, is the initiator of what God accomplished through the disciples. J. I. Packer stated it well:

> The Christian's life in all its aspects – intellectual and ethical, devotional and relational, upsurging in worship and outgoing in witness – is super-natural; only the Spirit can initiate and sustain it.[4]

The book of *Acts* reveals the Holy Spirit, not man, as the great initiator in the work of his church. Consider the following:

- It was the Holy Spirit, who birthed the first church (Acts 2).
- It was the Holy Spirit who empowered the first spokesman (preacher) of the early church (Acts 4:8).
- It was the Holy Spirit who gave believers the boldness to share their faith in Christ (Acts 4:31).
- It was the Holy Spirit who brought conviction and conversion to the first Gentile converts (Acts 10:44-45).
- It was the Holy Spirit (not a church board) who set apart the first missionary team (Acts 13:1-2).
- It was the Holy Spirit who helped the apostles decide a major debate among the Christians (Acts 15:28).
- It was the Holy Spirit who decided the apostles' itineraries (Acts 16:6-7).
- It was the Holy Spirit who chose elders in local churches (Acts 20:28).

One of the believer's greatest temptations is to neglect the Holy Spirit and take matters into our own hands. C.T. Studd, a man highly regarded in mission work, commented:

How little chance the Holy Ghost has nowadays. The churches and missionary societies have so bound Him in red tape that they practically ask Him to sit in a corner while they do the work themselves.[5]

God's children are not those who dictate to God, but rather those who are *led by the Spirit*.[6] We are warned not to *resist the Holy Spirit*[7]; not to *grieve the Holy Spirit*[8]; not to *insult the Holy Spirit*[9]; and not to *quench the Spirit*.[10] We can quench the Spirit in another believer or in ourselves. In a sense, we "pour cold water" on the Spirit when we become critical and resentful of others or stifle the prompting of the Spirit in ourselves. One version says, *Never damp the fire of the Spirit*.[11]

The book of *Galatians* was written to warn believers against neglecting the way of faith and the power of the Holy Spirit and reverting into man-made traditions and self-efforts: *Are you so foolish? After beginning with the Spirit, are you now trying to attain your goal by human effort?*[12] God's words to Zerubbabel echo this emphasis: *"Not by might nor by power, but by my Spirit," says the Lord Almighty.*[13] This Scripture should apply to our personal accomplishments that are done in the name of the Lord, as well as the work of the corporate church. M. Lloyd-Jones made a valid point:

> When the church operates in the power and strength of the Holy Spirit, it does more in one day than it would otherwise do through all its activities without the Spirit in years.[14]

A good test of how much church work depends on the Holy Spirit or only on man is simply: how well would this work do if this certain man were gone? If it "falls to pieces," then possibly the work is on a faulty foundation. A. W. Tozer put it even more bluntly:

> You can write it down as a fact: no matter what a man does, no matter how successful he seems to be in any field, if the Holy Spirit is not the chief energizer of his activity, it will all fall apart when he dies.[15]

Robert Girard suggested a principle which probably would not be welcomed today in many churches, but it would certainly contribute to the spiritual depth of any local body who practiced it:

> Anything in the church program that cannot be maintained without constant pastoral pressure on the people should be allowed to die a sure and natural death.[16]

The Deadly Danger of Traditionalism

What would happen in churches across the land if every pastor announced next Sunday morning, "I am not going to deliver a sermon because I sense that God wants us to take time now to pray for one another and to minister as the body of Christ?" Probably most congregations would be utterly shocked and not prepared to respond. Why? Because an old, established, and unbiblical tradition had just been tampered with.

Traditionalism includes the idea of being resistant to new changes, or being set in the old order of things. The Bible is not against tradition per se, because godly traditions of the past can be very important to our faith in the present (Communion is one example).[17] Traditionalism, however, is tradition for the sake of tradition, commanding excessive respect, even to the status of divine revelation. One author distinguishes between the two: "Tradition is the living faith of the dead, whereas traditionalism is the dead faith of the living."[18]

It is part of human nature to become comfortable, settled, and content with the status quo. The prophet Jeremiah reproved the people of Moab for this very reason:

They are like wine left to settle.
They have never been poured from one jar to another. . .
So they taste as they did before.
And their smell has not changed.[19]

Churches who think of themselves as being independent, charismatic, or free from denominationalism can sink into traditionalism as easily as any church. A church, for example, might proudly call itself a "New Testament church" and yet every Sunday morning meet in a church building until 12:00, have the same basic order of service, pass an offering plate, and hear sermons from the same man. None of these activities has any biblical basis; they are all traditions! This is not to say they are all bad, but the point is that almost all churches have some traditions. If we are not careful, we too can easily fall into mere, lifeless routines to which we unwittingly cling. J. I. Packer said,

> All Christians are at once beneficiaries and victims of tradition – beneficiaries, who receive nurturing truth and wisdom from God's faithfulness in past generations; victims, who now take for granted things that need to be questioned, thus treating as divine absolute patterns of belief and behavior that should be seen as human, provisional, and relative. We are all beneficiaries of good, wise, and sound tradition and victims of poor, unwise, and unsound traditions.[20]

All congregations must continually seek the Lord and bring their practices (some long established) under the scrutiny of the word and Spirit of God. We must dare to ask *why* we are doing what we are doing. The demons of hell cannot harm the word of God, but the traditions of men can rob it of its authority and bring it to no effect; Jesus said, *You nullify the word of God for the sake of your tradition.*[21] Another translation says, *So you have set aside what God has said for the sake of what has been handed down to you.*[22] A classic example of this is the tradition that only an ordained clergyman can do certain tasks in the church – e.g., baptize, serve communion, counsel, or give a sermon.

Flexibility is Needed in Our Meetings

Planning is certainly not against Scripture. We are exhorted to *love God with all our mind*[23] and *to make plans, counting on God to direct us.*[24] Our plans, however, both for ourselves and for the church should be *flexible.* There are pastors who plan out their messages four months in advance, more dictated by events on a calendar than the revealing of *the real need* in the church by the Holy Spirit. I have visited quite a number of churches (both charismatic and non-charismatic), and in most Sunday morning meetings, there is little flexibility in the format. Usually songs, Scripture readings, announcements, and a sermon are so well planned that even if the Holy Spirit wanted to do something different, he could not! Church leaders might justify this in the name of "order" or say that the Holy Spirit led them to make all their plans during the week. Michael Green, British theologian and evangelist, shared his impression:

> Most modern churches . . . don't need to be told that worship is ordered. They know it very well. It is often tightly shut, so tight that nobody could take part in it if it had not been prearranged, let alone the Holy Spirit.[25]

The New Testament idea of church meetings was quite different from most modern day meetings. In giving specific direction for church meetings, Paul encourages *all* to come prepared to *contribute*, not just to sit as spectators, while a few professionals perform. *Every* believer may potentially have something which could edify the others.

> *What then shall we say, brothers? When you come together, everyone has a hymn, or a word of instruction, a revelation, a tongue or an interpretation. All of these must be done for the strengthening of the church.*[26]

Paul is clear that the service should be orderly and not confusing,[27] but he also encourages flexibility:

> *But should a message of truth come to one who is seated, then the original speaker should stop talking. For in this way you can all have the opportunity to give a message, one after the other, and everyone will learn something and everyone will have his faith stimulated.*[28]

For the past ten years, I have shared the pastoral leadership with a few other men in a church of about three hundred. If you ever visit us, you will hopefully discover two things quickly: (1) we are far from being a perfect church, and (2) because of His unfathomable love and patience, God dwells among us. Our meetings are planned, since we have an organized worship team, structured teaching from gifted men, and an extensive children's ministry. However, in all our planning we want to give the body of Christ an opportunity to respond if the Holy Spirit nudges them. In most meetings we have some "open mike time" for anyone to contribute as the Spirit leads. We usually do not have to wait long; someone will bring a Scripture, someone else will give a testimony of God's protection, and yet another will share an encouraging answer to prayer. There have also been a few occasions when there were so many edifying words coming from different believers, that the planned message was "put on hold" until another meeting. The Holy Spirit in such times just seemed to "take over" with his own agenda. Oswald Chambers once said, "God takes great delight in breaking up our programs."[29] This type of meeting is quite risky for us who shepherd the flock, but we do not feel the meeting belongs to *us*. Sometimes we do have people speak words which do not seem very edifying or there are awkward times of silence. However, the good far outweighs the bad, and the group has been blessed by this kind of format.

The Gift of Piloting

Probably one of the most needed charismatic gifts of the Holy Spirit in our day, if we are willing to make room for it, is the gift of *piloting*. This may not be a recognizable gift at first, but it is listed in I Cor. 12:28 where most translations either translate it gifts of *administration* (NIV and NAS) or *governments* (KJV). The Greek word, however, means "a pilot, one who steers a ship." (The same word is used in Acts 27:11 of a pilot.) If our meetings are truly going to be led by the Holy Spirit, we will need men whose lives are hidden with Christ in God[30], and who are gifted to "pilot" a meeting, guiding and steering in the appropriate direction. This preferably will not be a singular leader as the gift is listed in the plural. A man with this gift may be an elder, a worship leader, or any willing brother. Whoever they are, these persons will be willing to step forward and provide direction as the Spirit prompts. One modern Bible version translated this gift as *power . . . to direct.*[31] Another translator says, *power . . . to guide.*[32] Gerhard Kittle, in his exhaustive Greek dictionary, made this comment: "The reference can only be to the specific gifts which qualify a Christian to be a helmsman to his congregation, i.e., a true director of its order and therewith of its life."[33]

God will use some with the gift of piloting to guide the general affairs of the church – i.e., in "steering" the group in a specific direction. This gift, like any gift of the Holy Spirit, should not just be limited to the context of church meetings. Every congregation, however, which desires the Holy Spirit to orchestrate its meetings, should pray earnestly for God to raise up several brethren who have this gift.

We All Have a Responsibility

If we truly desire our meetings to be led and filled with the Holy Spirit, then we all have a responsibility to come spiritually prepared.

> *So here's what I want you to do. When you gather together for worship, each one of you be prepared with something that will be useful to all: Sing a hymn, teach a lesson, tell a story, lead a prayer, provide an insight.*[34]

Church elders must be responsible for what takes place in meetings. Good shepherds will protect the flock. Occasionally we instruct the church how to participate in our "open mike" time. Some believers are too long-winded or do not know how to get to the point. The following are some guidelines we actually printed up for our church members.

GUIDELINES FOR TIMES OF SHARING TOGETHER IN OUR MEETINGS

Seek to abound for the edification of the church. (1 Cor. 14:12) *Let all things be done for edification.* (1 Cor. 14:26)

Following are two basic questions we must always ask if we share with the church: (1) Is it rooted in the word of God? and (2) Will it edify the church? The following are guidelines for any who speak during open mike time:

(1) Scripture reading is good. A few verses are better than lengthy passages.

(2) We encourage prophetic words. Unless you have a strong voice, come to the microphone. Prophecies may also be written out in advance and read on Sunday.

(3) Any personal testimonies should be brief unless an elder makes an exception. Sunday morning is not the best time for casually telling lengthy, detailed stories. Testimonies longer than five minutes are generally too long. Longer testimonies with more details may be better suited in small group settings. In sharing anything personally in the corporate meetings, we must quickly get to the point, and edify the church.

(4) There should be a clear-cut message in anything we share. *If the trumpet does not sound a clear call, who will get ready for battle?* (1 Cor. 14:8) If a testimony has confusing or controversial elements, or tends to ramble around many points, people may be confused and not understand clearly what is being communicated.

(5) Generally, it is good to share prayer requests during the worship time when the elders and others will be available for prayer, rather than during the general sharing time.

(6) Special songs, poems, or even skits may be shared, but it would be good to talk first to one of the elders about what you plan to do, and let them determine if it is appropriate.

(7) If ever in doubt, discuss your burden with an elder first. Also, sometimes it will be helpful to write down what you say.

(8) *Above all, love each other deeply, because love covers over a multitude of sins* (1 Peter 4:8). Because we are all learners in the Lord's school, we will all make mistakes. None of us will minister 100% in the Spirit of the Lord all the time. So, we can all be forbearing and patient with one another!

Let us be more open to the Holy Spirit to make a contribution to the corporate life of the church. William Barclay has left us with some powerful points to ponder, in his commentary on First Corinthians, chapter fourteen.

There was obviously a flexibility about the order of service in the early Church. Everything was informal enough to allow any man who felt that he had a message to give to give it. It may well be that we set far too much store on dignity and order nowadays, and have become the slaves of orders of service. The really notable thing about an early Church service must have been that almost everyone came feeling that he had both the privilege and the obligation of contributing something to it. A man did not come with the sole intention of being a passive listener; he came not only to receive but to give.

Obviously this had its dangers, for it is clear that in Corinth there were those who were too fond of the sound of their own voices; but nonetheless the Church

123

must have been in those days much more the real possession of the ordinary Christian. It may well be that the Church lost something when she delegated so much to the professional ministry and left so little to the ordinary Church member; and it may well be that the blame lies not with the ministry for annexing those rights but with the laity for abandoning them. Certainly it is all too true that many Church members think far more of what the Church can do for them than of what they can do for the Church, and are very ready to criticize what is done but very unready to take any share in doing the Church's work themselves.[35]

Chapter Eleven
Properly Assessing
Ministries in the Church

It was he who gave some to be apostles, some to be prophets,
some to be evangelists, and some to be pastors and teachers,
to prepare God's people for works of service, so that the
body of Christ may be built up until we all reach unity
in the faith and in the knowledge of the Son of God and
become mature, attaining to the whole measure of the
fullness of Christ.[1]

This is a key passage concerning development in the church.
First of all, we see God has given specific ministry gifts to the body
of Christ to help us mature. Second, the ministry gifts themselves
are not to do all the work of the ministry; they are to equip us –
the members of the body – to do the work of ministry.

In this book, we cannot adequately describe these four or
five ministry gifts. (Some combine the pastor-teacher into one
calling.) Most emphasis in the church today is on the role of the
pastor/teacher. Yet, if the church is going to mature and attain to
the whole measure of the fullness of Christ, we will likely see more
emphasis in the future on the apostle, prophet, and evangelist
being connected with the local church. There are entire books
which deal more thoroughly with these three ministry gifts, so I
will defer to them.[2] I would simply define these gifts as follows:

• Apostle – A church planter (some "missionaries" may actually be apostles); a "master-builder" who lays the foundation of Jesus Christ in the church; a spiritual father who has an extensive influence over a larger segment of the body of Christ.

• Prophet – A man who has keen insight into the present plans and purposes of God. This man carries a burden – a "now" word for the church. He may have insights into the future, but his ministry will primarily bring a dimension of Spirit-inspired comfort, edification, and exhortation.

• Evangelist – A man who is strongly burdened to reach the lost. He will be effective in connecting with an audience targeted by the Holy Spirit. He will also motivate the body of Christ to get out of their "comfort zones" and reach out to the lost world.

• Pastor/teacher – A man who has a greater burden for the local congregation. He is a shepherd who cares for the sheep in his fold. As a teacher he desires to instruct both new Christians and older ones from the "whole counsel of God" – truths which lead to maturity and greater Christlikeness.

If the church is going to develop into all that God intends, we must be open to all of these ministry gifts. However, as we know, there have been many who have come in the name of an "apostle," "prophet," etc. who have wreaked much havoc in the body of Christ. At a pastors' conference in India I recently asked, "Suppose a man came to you and said, 'I am a prophet sent by God and I have a message for your congregation.' How many of you would let him speak to your church?" About half the group raised their hands, indicating a "yes." I then proceeded to instruct them about . . .

The Necessity of Judging Ministries

Keep watch over yourselves and all the flock of which the Holy Spirit has made you overseers. Be shepherds of the church of God, which he bought with his own blood. I know that after I leave, savage wolves will come in among you and will not spare the flock. Even from your own number men will arise and distort the truth in order to draw away disciples after them. So be on your guard![3]

Some believers are hesitant to judge others because Jesus said, *"Judge not, lest you be judged."* However, Jesus is guarding against a critical spirit, not from exercising discernment (see Matt. 7:1-5). We are to deal with any critical or angry attitudes first (*"the log in our own eye"*). Then we can deal with the sin (*"the splinter"*) in our brother's eye. This same chapter encourages us to be discerning and make proper judgments: *Watch out for false prophets. They come to you in sheep's clothing, but inwardly they are ferocious wolves. By their fruit you will recognize them"* (Matt. 7:15-16). So, if we are going to *watch out for false prophets,* some judgment is needed!

Pastors are the shepherds of the flock. In ancient days the shepherd slept in front of the rectangular pen in which he kept his sheep. No wolf could go into the sheepfold without first going through the shepherd.[4] Therefore, the local pastors are responsible for any ministry that takes place in their congregation.

The only gateway to the sheepfold was guarded by good shepherds.

The following are some guidelines in judging ministries in a responsible manner.

1. Realize that local pastors/elders are the authority in the local church.

Sometimes traveling "apostles," "prophets," or "teachers" will come in and try to override the local pastors/elders or take over a church meeting. Local pastors/elders are God's authority in the local church. Any true apostle or prophet or traveling teacher ought to be a part of a local body of believers, be "sent out" from that group, and be able to return and give an account of his ministry.[5] Anyone who desires to minister publically in the name of Christ must also be willing to be judged by the local leaders of the church in which he ministers. Scripture is clear about this.

> *You have tested those who claim to be apostles but are not, and have found them false.*[6]

> *And let two or three prophets speak, and let the others pass judgment. . . . If anyone thinks he is a prophet or spiritual, let him recognize that the things which I write to you are the Lord's commandment. But if anyone does not recognize this, he is not recognized.*[7]

> *For a time is coming when people will no longer listen to right teaching. They will follow their own desires and will look for teachers who will tell them whatever they want to hear. They will reject the truth and follow strange myths.*[8]

When I am invited into other congregations to teach, I go humbly as a servant to that church. Our attitude as guests should not be to *lord it over your faith; rather we are workers with you for your joy.*[9] We should not teach in any way to undermine their leadership. If I am invited to teach a pastors' seminar in another country, I first send my teaching outlines to the brethren in charge and ask for their input. As I minister, I also invite any correction from them if they detect anything amiss in my spirit or message.

2. Don't be naive; it never hurts to "check things out."

The Greek verb, *to judge*, comes from three different words with the following meanings: "to undergo process of trial, give sentence, condemn, execute judgment upon, govern, form an opinion, to make a resolve, examine, question, and investigate carefully."[10] Christians are called to believe the best of others,[11] but this does not mean we never raise questions or "check things out," especially when we hear Bible teaching that does not seem right. *A simple man believes every word he hears; a clever man understands the need for proof.*[12] Even if the Christian worker is a so-called "expert" and you are a brand new Christian, you have the responsibility to *test everything. Hold on to the good.*[13]

3. Know those who will labor among you.

A pastor generally should not allow anyone whom he does not personally know to preach or influence the congregation. Just because someone else has highly recommended an outside ministry does not mean we automatically "open the door." Scripture says we should *know those who will labor among you.*[14] I know one pastor friend who gave a stranger opportunity to speak to his congregation. The first half of his message seemed good, but then for the entire second half, the speaker gave an impassioned appeal for money to be given to his ministry. Sometimes we learn through bad experiences!

4. Realize no one is immune to correction.

Some workers think they are immune to correction and judgment from other believers and will even quote David's words, *"Touch not mine anointed."*[15] King David was indeed called *God's anointed,*[16] and yet he received advice from his friend Jonathan;[17] reproof from the prophet Nathan;[18] and even when an enemy, Shimei, cursed the king, David was amazingly receptive: *"If the Lord has told him to curse me, who am I to say no?"*[19] No Christian worker should be above correction. An elderly servant of the Lord, John Wright Follette, remarked, "In regard to dealing with a wayward minister, I feel I am not touching the Lord's anointed; I am correcting a piece of flesh."[20]

5. We should be very cautious when Christian workers seem motivated by money.

Probably more than any other, greed is a dynamic which will characterize a false prophet or teacher. Balaam was a gifted prophetic man, yet he was strongly rebuked because he encouraged immorality and he *loved the wages of wickedness.*[21] Greed is a subtle temptation for servants of God, and those who minister in his name must guard their hearts. Watchman Nee echoed this concern in his writing on the local church:

> The greatest test for a false apostle is money. Whoever is not clear of money and harbors the ulterior motive of gain in his heart is doubtless a false apostle. A false apostle will be one who either seeks for fame or for wealth . . . Whenever money has its hold on us, our work shall cease to be wholly for the Lord.[22]

Some of the teachers who have impressed me the most are those who are not overly concerned about any profit they make. I do not think that those who make money from books, tapes, or lectures are false teachers, but this is a spiritually dangerous area. Some traveling Christian speakers stipulate they will not speak to audiences less than five hundred. Why? What motivates such a stipulation? I have also heard of some Christian leaders charging over a thousand dollars to speak on a single night. Why? Can we imagine the apostles Peter or John charging a group the equivalent of a thousand dollars to bring a message from God? We are urged in Scripture to care for God's flock in a manner *not greedy for money, but eager to serve.*[23] We should avoid any teacher who over-emphasizes the money element. Jesus knows how our hearts are susceptible to greed in a multitude of manifestations: *Watch out! Be on your guard against all kinds of greed.*[24] Martyn Lloyd-Jones gives a warning we should all take to heart:

> These earthly treasures are so powerful that they grip the entire personality. They grip a man's heart, his mind and his will; they tend to affect his spirit, his soul and his whole being. Whatever realm of life we may be looking at, or thinking about, we shall find these things are there. Everyone is affected by them; they are a terrible danger.[25]

6. We are to judge the spirits behind religious movements and experiences.
Dear friends, do not believe every spirit, but test the spirits to see whether they are from God, because many false prophets have gone into the world.[26]

But the Spirit explicitly says that in later times some will fall away from the faith, paying attention to deceitful spirits and doctrines of demons.[27]

A charismatic gift we desperately need in our day is the *distinguishing of spirits.*[28] We have seen quite a number of things going on – e.g., folks being "slain in the Spirit," dancing before the Lord, shaking, "holy laughter," and so on. Some of these expressions may be legitimate, but questions ought to be asked; and we should not hesitate to judge such experiences properly. Behind any religious experience may be the Holy Spirit, the human spirit, or a demonic spirit.[29] This is true of most spiritual gifts and experiences. It does not hurt to put things to the test. We are being spiritually negligent if we do not. Someone has rightly said, "Truth never fears examination."

How are we to test the spirits? Jonathan Edwards saw quite a bit of spiritual activity – both good and bad – in the First

Great Awakening. Edwards wisely encouraged discernment. In his book *The Distinguishing Marks of a Work of the Spirit of God*,[30] he listed the following five questions to apply to any spiritual manifestation or experience:

- Does it exalt Jesus Christ as Son of God and Savior, leading people to honor Him as such?
- Does it oppose Satan's kingdom by weaning people from sin, lust and worldliness?
- Does it teach people to revere and trust the Bible as the Word of God?
- Does it make people feel the urgency of eternal issues and the depth of their own lostness without Christ?
- Does it stir up in people new love of Christ and others?

One more crucial test for spiritual experiences is the test of humility. A. W. Tozer explained this test:

> A good rule is this: if this experience has served to humble me and make me little and vile in my own eyes, it is of God; but if it has given me a feeling of self-satisfaction, it is false and should be dismissed as emanating from self or the devil. Nothing that comes from God will minister to my pride or self-congratulation. If I am tempted to be complacent and to feel superior because I have had a remarkable vision or an advanced spiritual experience, I should go at once to my knees and repent of the whole thing. I have fallen victim to the enemy.[31]

Let us remember that the church is not our own; it is *the church of God, which he bought with his own blood.*[32] Let us do all we can to protect the precious bride of Christ and see it come to greater maturity, even *attaining to the whole measure of the fullness of Christ.*[33]

Chapter Twelve
Practical Outworkings of Church Unity

All our talk about church unity is only theoretical if it is not worked out in the nitty-gritty life of a local church. The local church has been rightly called "God's workshop." In the building of God's spiritual house, the many "living stones" must be chiseled by the Lord to fit together properly. The New Testament uses the expression, *one another*, over thirty times, indicating there is to be much interaction in the body of Christ. Let us look at several practical ways we can demonstrate unity in the local assembly.

Accepting One Another

May the God who gives endurance and encouragement give you a spirit of unity among yourselves as you follow Jesus Christ. . . . Accept one another, then, just as Christ accepted you . . .[1]

If we fully realized that every sincere, born-again believer is a brother or sister in Christ, we would surely act differently. The basis of Christian unity is the fact that every true Christian has the same Father and is part of one big family. Albert Barnes explained:

Christ did not come to redeem and save different churches and to give them a different place in heaven. . . . He did not come to save merely the black man, or the red, or the white man; nor did he leave the world to set up for them separate mansions in the skies. He came that he might collect into one community a multitude of every complexion, and from every land, and unite them in one great brotherhood on earth, and ultimately assemble them in the same heaven. The church is one. Every sincere Christian is a brother in that church and has an equal right with all others to its privileges. . . . Every Christian, no matter what his rank, should be ready to hail every other Christian as a fellow-heir of heaven.[2]

The word *brothers* or *brethren* occurs some 250 times in the New Testament. We can be brethren by PLACE (having the same country or nation[3]); we can be brethren by RACE (having the same parents[4]); or we can be brethren by GRACE (having a supernatural regeneration[5]). We are commanded to *love the brotherhood of believers.*[6]

When we become a part of the body of Christ, we will learn quickly that there are many different kinds of brethren! We are a varied people of God through whom God will show to the rulers and authorities in heavenly places the *manifold wisdom of God.*[7] The expression *manifold* in the Greek language means, "much variegated; marked with a great variety of colors; much varied; manifesting itself in a great variety of forms."[8] The Greek word is only used in this one place in the New Testament, but the same root word is used in the Septuagint (Greek) Old Testament to describe Joseph's coat of many colors.[9] In Joseph's day typical colors of clothing were solid, so his coat of many colors was a radical departure from the norm. Throughout history God has displayed through the church his variegated wisdom to the universe. Different groups – past and present – have displayed unique hues, tints, and shades of the wisdom of God. This incredible variety is not just for the future, when the church will finally be perfect; it is for the church today:

> *In order that now, through the church, the wisdom of God in its infinite variety might be made known to the rulers and authorities in the heavenly realms . . .*[10]

When we become part of a local church, it is like becoming part of a big family. One author gets more specific:

> I envision the church being something like a big Italian family where there is no shortage of difference of opinion and heated conflict. Sometimes big fights break out and neighbors shudder, wondering whether the family will stay together. But when an outsider attacks one of its members, the family pulls together, stands as one and defends its own. Loyalty undergirds it. They might not always get along, but they still know to what family they belong.[11]

In a normal, natural family, members differ, but because they belong to each other, they work out their problems through "thick and thin." We must learn to accept all brethren and give each other a little more "spiritual breathing room."

> *After all, who are you to criticize the servant of somebody else, especially when that somebody else is God?*[12]

Appreciating One Another

Different churches will have distinct ministries or emphases. Just as no two thumbprints are alike, every local church will be unique, with different leaders, different forms of service, different styles of worship, and different corporate personalities. We should appreciate these differences. Paul and Peter had two entirely different ministries, yet Paul saw the hand of God in both:

> *For God, who was at work in the ministry of Peter as an apostle to the Jews, was also at work in my ministry as an apostle to the Gentiles.*[13]

Paul recognized that he had a particular *sphere of influence* determined by the Lord.[14] God also establishes a *sphere of influence* for individual churches. Not every church needs to start a Christian school. Not every church needs to be involved in a mission to the poor. Not every church needs to reach out to Jews. We should respect different emphases. Remember Jesus' words: *Do not hinder him; for he who is not against you is for you.*[15]

There are built-in differences and tensions which are good for the body of Christ. Derek Prince described the body in this way:

> Muscles are activities or ministries of the Body; oddly enough, *muscles in the body work against each other.* In other words, some muscles bend my arm while others extend it. So it is in the body of Christ, the activities of the body work in tension, some bending, and some extending as the body moves. The secret of the body's activity is the tension within it. Properly balanced tensions make the body function. Unbalanced tensions paralyze it.[16]

MOST MUSCLES WORK IN PAIRS. For example: when the muscle in the front of the upper arm contracts, the triceps in the back of the arm relaxes (see arm on left). The contraction of the biceps bends the arm toward the shoulder. When the triceps contract (see arm on right), the biceps relax and the arm straightens.[17]

Different gifted people will sometimes clash and either of them can become unbalanced, without checks and balances in the body. Some examples of counterbalancing tensions in the body of Christ might include:

- **Traveling evangelists vs. Pastors**

The evangelists say, "People are dying and going to hell; we need to get out with the gospel!" The pastor says, "We need to stay here and take care of the sheep!"

- **Worship leaders vs. Bible teachers**

Some worship leaders seem to get caught up in the Lord's presence; an hour has gone by, and they are just getting started! They say, "Don't quench the Spirit!" The Bible teacher, on the other hand, is getting anxious and looking at the clock – "We can't neglect the word!"

- **Visionary vs. Pragmatic**

This conflict will usually emerge when a congregation makes a big financial decision, like purchasing a building. The "visionary" is the man full of faith who says, "Let's go for it!" The pragmatic man will be more cautious and will want to carefully "count the cost" before proceeding.

- **The Prophet vs. the Administrator**

The prophetic brother will want to "sense what the Spirit is saying," before taking any action. The administrator will say, "We need to carefully plan this thing out."

- **Compassionate vs. Corrective**

The difference in these gifts will be seen when a member of the body has fallen in sin. The person with the gift of mercy will be more interested in helping the hurting and showing the Lord's compassion to all – even the undeserving. He will gently hug the offender, "Oh, brother, I feel for you. I'm sure I could have done the same thing!" The brother with the gift of exhortation, however, will want to correct anything amiss. He will have no tolerance for sin; his message is very simple, "Repent! Turn from that sin and get right with God – now!"

In each conflict, which group is right? Possibly both. Even though each group may justify its position with Scripture passages, we need to realize that there are sometimes different facets of one truth. Because we are human and not entirely without prejudice, we tend to emphasize those passages which favor our positions, and minimize or ignore those passages which do not. Most great doctrines in Scripture have a balancing truth and both facets may be necessary for the knowledge of whole truth. Derek Prince said:

> Instead of bemoaning the presence of these differences in the body, let us thank God that He has placed them there. Without counterbalancing tensions, the Body of Christ is swiftly on its way to paralysis.[18]

Some weaker brethren will develop strong opinions on certain diets, special days to observe, dress, political issues, or entertainment. We do need to encourage modesty, godliness, and keeping a Christlike testimony. However, on non-essentials, it is good to go the extra mile for unity and accept one another:

> *Accept him whose faith is weak, without passing judgment on disputable matters. . . . Therefore let us stop passing judgment on one another. Instead make up your mind not to put any stumbling block or obstacle in your brother's way. . . . It is better not to eat meat or drink wine or to do anything that will cause your brother to fall.*
>
> *May the God who gives endurance and encouragement give you a spirit of unity among yourselves as you follow Christ Jesus . . .*[19]

Walking Humbly with One Another

Paul's great chapter on church unity, Ephesians Four, begins with these words:

> *Be completely humble and gentle; be patient, bearing with one another in love. Make every effort to keep the unity of the Spirit through the bond of peace . . .*

Without humility there is little hope for unity. R. C. Chapman said, "Humility is the secret of fellowship, and pride the secret of division."[20] Matthew Henry called pride, "the cause of most dissensions and breaches in the church."[21] This agrees with Solomon's words: *By pride comes only contention.*[22]

The humble man will think little of himself and be more tolerant of others. The proud man will likely be overly critical and suspicious of others, and thereby keep his distance. John Calvin said,

> Humility is the first step to unity. . . . The man is truly humble who never claims any personal merit in the sight of God, nor proudly despises brethren, or aims at being superior to them, but reckons it enough that he is one of the members of Christ, and desires nothing more than that the Head alone should be exalted.[23]

In his book, *Thoughts on the Revival in New England*, Jonathan Edwards judged pride to be the greatest single cause of the miscarriage of revivals. He comments:

> Spiritual pride is very apt to suspect others; whereas an humble saint is most jealous of himself, he is so suspicious of nothing in the world as he is of his own heart. The spiritually proud person is apt to find fault with other saints, that they are low in grace; and to

be much in observance how cold and dead they are; and being quick to discern and take notice of their deficiencies. But the eminently humble Christian has much to do at home . . .[24]

The humble Christian will not dwell on the faults of other believers and will realize his own shortcomings. The humble church will have interaction with other Christian bodies, avoiding any unspoken attitude of being "God's defender of the truth," or, even worse, "We are too holy for you."

We need to recognize our need for one another; we cannot say, *I have no need of you.*[25] Edwards continues describing the humble Christian:

And though he will not be a companion with one that is visibly Christ's enemy . . . yet he does not love the appearance of an open separation from visible Christians . . . and will as much as possible shun all appearance of a superiority, or distinguishing himself as better than others.[26]

It will require a humble spirit to take a genuine interest in other believers outside of ourselves: *Do nothing out of selfish ambition or vain conceit, but in humility consider others better than yourselves. Each of you should look not only to your own interests, but also to the interests of others.*[27]

Forgiving One Another

I once read of two unmarried sisters who lived together, but because of an unresolved disagreement over an insignificant issue, they had stopped speaking to each another. Since they were either unable or unwilling to move out of their small house, they continued to use the same rooms, eat at the same table, use the same appliances, and sleep in the same room . . . all separately . . .

without one word. A chalk line divided the sleeping area in half, separating doorways as well as fireplace. Each would come and go, cook and eat, sew and read without ever stepping over into her sister's territory. Through the black of the night, each could hear the deep breathing of the other, but because both were unwilling to take the first step toward forgiving and forgetting the silly offense, they coexisted for years in grinding silence.[28]

This pathetic story aptly illustrates the results of a refusal to forgive. There will be no true unity in a local church if members are not walking in forgiveness. C. S. Lewis once said, "Everyone says forgiveness is a lovely idea, until they have something to forgive . . ."[29] Sometimes those closest to us will do or say unkind things. They may falsely accuse us or unjustly criticize our congregation. Those who seriously follow Jesus will have ample opportunity to practice forgiveness. *Bear with each other and forgive whatever grievances you may have against one another. Forgive as the Lord forgave you.*[30]

What is forgiveness? We normally think of it as "to pardon, cancel, or remit," but in the Greek language it is a word which has a much broader meaning. It also means "to leave it, tolerate, abandon, let go, disregard and not to discuss now."[31] When we say, "I forgive you," we are saying, "I am leaving you with the Lord." That person who rubs us the wrong way may be as wrong as wrong can be, but we are leaving his judgment with God, not taking matters into our hands. Someone has said, "Forgiveness is surrendering my right to hurt you for hurting me." In most congregations, because there is such a diverse group of people, it is quite easy to be offended or hurt by another. However, no believer has a right to hold on to hurts. We are to follow in the footsteps of Jesus: *When they hurled their insults at him, he did not retaliate; when he suffered, he made not threats. Instead, he entrusted himself to him who judges justly.*[32] The Christian is called not only to endure hurts and unjust criticism, but to even *love your enemies, do good to those who hate you, bless those who curse you, pray for those who mistreat you.*[33]

Many a church has been divided and hurt significantly because one individual stubbornly refused to forgive those who offended him. Unforgiveness is one of the greatest enemies of Christian love and unity. When we forgive, we do as the Lord has done for us, we wipe the slate clean: *Love . . . keeps no record of wrongs.*[34] Forgiveness is not something we will necessarily feel like doing, but it is a matter of the heart and a decision to love.[35] Forgiveness is also a commitment to forget. Amy Carmichael says,

> If I say, "Yes, I forgive, but I cannot forget," as though the God who twice a day washes all the sands on all the shores of all the world, could not wash such memories from my mind, then I know nothing of Calvary love.[36]

It is true that some painful memories such as abuse incurred as a child may be hard to forget. If we truly forgive, however, we can avoid dwelling on those thoughts when they come. *Webster's Dictionary* says to forget means, "to lose the remembrance of; to treat with inattention or disregard; to neglect; to cease noticing."[37] When our Lord Jesus forgives our sins, He promises to forget them: *I will remember their sins no more.*[38] Christian counselor Jay Adams says we must forgive in the same way:

> When you forgive another, you declare that you are canceling his debt, removing his guilt, and promising that you will never again bring up his offenses to use against him. This promise involves three things:
> 1. I will not bring the matter up to you.
> 2. I will not bring the matter up to another.
> 3. I will not bring the matter up to myself.[39]

When someone has hurt us deeply, this kind of commitment to forget requires supernatural grace along with our willingness. We see this demonstrated in Joseph, who was betrayed and sold into slavery by his brothers. Later in Egypt Joseph had two sons;

the first he named *Manasseh*, which means "making to forget" and the second, *Ephraim*, which means "fruitfulness."[40] When Joseph explained his presence in Egypt, he mentioned nothing about his brothers' cruel betrayal; he only said, "*I was forcibly carried off . . .*"[41] Joseph forgave his brothers to such an extent that he refused to dwell on what they had done. His naming of his sons indicates he chose to forget; as a result he became fruitful.

George Washington Carver was another man who learned forgiveness this way. He was once refused admission to a university because he was black. Years later, when someone asked him the name of the university, he replied, "Never mind. That doesn't matter now."[42] Through this kind of forgiveness, Carver demonstrated the Spirit of Jesus. This forgiving spirit will do much to preserve unity and express a testimony of our Lord. Someone has defined forgiveness as "the fragrance the blossom leaves on the heel of the boot that crushes it."

Forbearing One Another

Another practical way we grow in unity is by having opportunities to forbear one another.

With all humility and gentleness, with patience, showing forbearance to one another in love, being diligent to preserve the unity of the Spirit in the bond of peace.[43]

To forbear our brethren is to show a gentle and patient attitude toward folks with whom we normally would have little to do. Forbear means "to put up with."[44] The Amplified Bible in the above verse says, *bearing with one another and making allowances because you love one another.*[45]

God will often send people into our churches who need a lot of help:

- Those whose personalities rub us the wrong way;
- Those with unseemly table manners or goofy humor;
- Those with self-sensitive dispositions who only talk about themselves and their problems;
- Those self-appointed experts who think they have the right answer to every problem;
- Those bossy volunteers; and
- Those with unattractive physical or mental qualities.

Our natural tendency will be to avoid these people, but God calls us to love them. It would be a wonderful thing if we could love all God's people, as Robert C. Chapman encouraged in his hymn:

Thy brethren, Lord, are my delight,
    I love them strong or weak;
They are all precious in my sight,
    The froward with the meek.

I serve them, Lord, for they are Thine,
    The Father's gift to Thee;
Thy Spirit, by Thy Blood divine,
    From prison set them free.

And still the froward ones I serve –
    Thy members, Lord, are they;
Hold Thou me up, nor let me swerve
    From Love's excelling way.[46]

Among Christians whom we deeply respect, as we become better acquainted, we may begin to notice certain flaws. If we are not careful, these apparent deficiencies may be a stumbling

144

block to our own spiritual walk. One thing that will help us is to remember how much God has shown forbearance to us, as Gerald Sittser has written.

> We have benefitted more than we know from God's forbearance. If we saw ourselves as God sees us, we would fall over dead with shame or fall at God's feet in utter devotion. We would discover how much time, space and opportunity God has given us to outgrow our immaturity. God calls us to imitate him in forbearing one another. He commands us to give each other the slack that he has given us. Forbearance thus requires that we give people room – room to be who they are, to become what God intends, to contribute what they can to the church and the world, in spite of their imperfections.[47]

Forbearance does not mean we tolerate sin or spiritual compromise. There is indeed a time to rightly judge sin in the body of Christ, and failure to do so will reap serious consequences on any church family.[48] However, we need to have the heart of God toward imperfect people. As God reveals more about our own soul, it makes us much more tolerant of others' flaws and shortcomings. It is appropriate to close this chapter with these words of wisdom from Charles Spurgeon.

> Every head has a soft place in it, and every heart has its black drop. Every rose has its prickles, and every day its night. Even the sun shows spots, and the skies are darkened with clouds. . . . The best wine has its dregs . . .
>
> Blessed is he who expects nothing of poor flesh and blood, for he shall never be disappointed. The best of men are men at best, and the best wax will melt. . . . The straightest timber has knots in it, and the cleanest

field of wheat has its share of weeds. . . . Since we all live in glass houses, then none of us should throw stones.[49]

Chapter Thirteen
The Love of God – the Perfect Bond of Unity

Beyond all these things put on love,
which is the perfect bond of unity.[1]

Two different objects which normally would have little attraction for one another can be strongly bound together by the right kind of glue. God has given us the "right kind of glue" – His own supernatural love dwelling in our hearts. God's love has the potential to bind all Christians together in unity.

We are Christ's only representatives in a wicked world; we need to put Christian love ahead of our strong opinions and divisive discussions. The love of Christ in our midst should take precedence over our doctrinal distinctives and personal preferences. Our "oneness in spirit" must practically be demonstrated through the love that Christ has shed abroad in our hearts. Andrew Murray comments:

> The hidden unity of life must be manifest in the visible unity and fellowship of love. Most believers consider it impossible to live in the full oneness of love with the children of God around them. Only when they learn that a life in love to each other is their simple duty, and begin to cry to God for His Holy Spirit to work it in them, will there be hope of change in this respect.[2]

In the family of God it is important that we learn to love because we are going to be spending more time together in eternity with brethren we hardly speak to now, than with our closest friends in the present life! Brothers in the same family may not always see things the same way, but they must never forget they are still brothers. Paul Billheimer wrote,

> There is only one answer to division over non-essentials and that is growth in love, agape love, and it will never come any other way. . . . God is more interested in love between members of His family than in the inerrancy of one's opinions.[3]

Scripture says, *Love does not insist on its own rights or its own way.*[4] In the end, our strong opinions or insistence on being right probably will not matter that much. Love is what will stand the Divine test, as Juan Carlos Ortiz illustrates:

> Imagine a man trying to sell his dairy farm. A buyer comes and notices something odd – the cows are separating in six or eight groups. He asks why.
> "Oh, we're very organized here," says the farmer. "These cows in this group have shorter legs."
> "I see. But the ones in that group have short legs also."
> "Yes, but those short-legged cows have longer tails," replied the farmer.
> "Ah. But the group over there has cows with short legs and long tails too. Why are they separate?"
> "Because they have long horns."
> "Of course. Now that bunch over there has short legs, long tails and long horns. Why are they apart?"
> "Because they're white." says the farmer.

Our divisions are just as silly as the farmer's. When we die, there will be only two groups: those who loved one another and those who didn't – the sheep and the goats. God will not be checking a big list of kosher groups and unkosher groups. He will be interested in those who accepted him and shared his love with others. *For I was hungry and you gave Me something to eat; I was thirsty, and you gave Me drink; I was a stranger, and you invited Me in; naked and you clothed me; I was sick and you visited Me; I was in prison, and you came to Me* (Matt. 25:35-36).

If there is any kind of standard God will look at, this is it: *We know that we have passed out of death into life, because we love the brethren* (I John 3:14).[5]

Love makes the difference. The love of God is far greater than any measure of human love. It will enable us to love those we would normally reject – even to love the unlovely. God's love will enable us to love even when we are not loved back. It will enable us to cover a multitude of sins that others would delight in exposing. Our love for one another (or lack of it) will be detected in our words, our inner attitudes, and our expectations of one another.

When I became a Christian, one change that convinced me of the reality of my conversion was that I immediately had a new love for people from a variety of backgrounds. Physical appearances, racial distinctives, and social status no longer made any difference to me. The love of God transcended all these former barriers. At times, I have been amazed at the love of God manifested through me, despite my human deficiencies.

After thirty-five years of relating to a multitude of God's people from many states as well as foreign countries, I have indeed met quite a variety in the family of God. I have learned that God's love will enlarge our hearts and adjust our attitudes when we become too critical or stand aloof. God's love will grant us a gentle, patient, and forbearing spirit toward those who are naturally unlovable. God's love will help us go the extra mile in times of strife and division.

Proper Attitudes When We Differ and Divide

What are we to do in times when we differ and, because neither side gives way, we are at an impasse with one another? There is only one thing we can do – we can choose to love! George Whitefield, who walked through some difficult times of differing with other brothers, offered this advice:

> Why should we dispute, when there is no probability of convincing? . . . I am persuaded that the more the love of God is shed abroad in our hearts, the more all narrowness of spirit will subside and give way. Besides, so far as we are narrow-spirited we are uneasy. Prejudices, jealousies and suspicions make the soul miserable.[6]

Love is the building material the Master Builder uses to build His church: *The whole body . . . grows and builds itself up in love.*[7] Our churches may have excellent Bible teaching, charismatic gifts, and sacrificial service; yet *without love, we are nothing.*[8] Jesus has given us a preeminent command: not just to love, but *to love as I have loved you.*[9] This means unity is much more than the absence of division and strife; it involves loving one another as the Father has loved the Son and as the Son has loved the Father. It means learning to love what Jesus Himself loves – the entire body of Christ. This dimension of love is what will draw an unsaved world to the Christ we profess.

It is inevitable that most of us will experience times of congregational stress and possibly even division. How we respond in such times is of vital importance for the protection and preservation of a local body. The following are three attitudes that should profoundly impact such situations for God's glory:

1. We can walk in a spirit of meekness.[10]

A co-pastor I knew in another church resigned because of unresolved differences between himself and the other pastor. Most of these differences revolved around the overall structure of leadership and future direction of the church. As I met with this man shortly after his resignation, I was impressed by his spirit of meekness. In the course of our conversation, he said nothing to belittle his fellow pastor and, in fact, spoke highly of him and the influence of that man in his life. This pastor had also informed the congregation that if anyone came to him with the intention of saying anything derogatory about his former co-pastor, he would hear none of it. In this particular parting of ways I saw a Christ-like attitude in both of these pastors, little mention of "rightness" or "wrongness," and as a result, little harm to the body of Christ. Over twenty years after the incident, God is still prospering the ministries of both men.

Meekness is a Greek word rich in meaning; no single English word can translate it. The Greek word, *praus*, can mean "gentle," "pleasant," "mild," or "soothing."[11] The word describes the quiet and friendly composure which does not become embittered or angry at what is unpleasant, whether in the form of people or circumstances.[12] These qualities would be helpful in the midst of any church division.

Volumes could be written about believers rejecting each other or those who have slipped into sin and have subsequently been harshly rejected without love or meekness by a church group. Sin in the church needs to be addressed in a straight-forward manner, but only with a meek and patient spirit.

> *God's people must not be quarrelsome; they must be gentle, patient teachers of those who are wrong. Be humble when you are trying to teach those who are mixed-up concerning the truth. For if you talk meekly and courteously to them they are more likely, with God's help, to turn away from their wrong ideas and believe what is true.*[13]

151

In church disagreements, we see a lot about people's level of spiritual maturity. We can either selfishly insist on our way or we can meekly trust God and defer to one another. If we cannot defer in a spirit of meekness, we are failing to walk in God's love: *Love . . . does not insist on its own way . . . Be devoted to one another in brotherly love; give preference to one another in honor.*[14]

We see a spirit of meekness in Abraham when he separated from Lot. Instead of fighting for his rights, this man of faith deferred to his nephew. When Abraham's family became crowded in a parcel of land shared with his nephew Lot, their herdsmen began quarreling, and Abraham decided it would be best to split apart and settle in different regions. He allowed Lot to take first pick and choose the best-looking land. Abraham, the elder of the two, could have easily insisted on first choice; he could have said, "Lot, you know I am the one to whom God speaks and I am the one He has chosen to father a great nation. Now step aside and let me choose . . ." No, Abraham deferred to his nephew and, as a result, ended up settling in God's chosen land.[15]

2. We can guard our tongues.

Our local church has had two times of major stress and division, which we have weathered by the grace of God. Looking back, the most damage was incurred through ugly and unkind words that were spoken. It seems that this is a favorite tool of the devil, especially in times of division. In stressful times believers may be too quick to judge amiss, to speak a wrong opinion, or to accuse one another falsely. If we can guard our tongues when we disagree or divide, we will do good to the body of Christ. Francis Schaeffer shared this excellent advice,

> If, when we feel we must disagree as true Christians, we could simply guard our tongues and speak in love, in five or ten years the bitterness could be gone. Instead of that, we leave scars – a curse for generations. Not just a curse in the church, but a curse in the world.

Newspaper headlines bear it in our Christian press, and it boils over into the secular press at times – Christians saying such bitter things about other Christians.[16]

Two men who are an example in history to the rest of the church are John Wesley and George Whitefield. These two eighteenth-century contemporaries were both used mightily of God in their independent ministries and each made a major contribution in the history of the church. The two men in their early days of ministry, however, separated because of theological differences – Whitefield's strong stand on election; Wesley's on sanctification. For many years they had little to do with each other, even speaking against each other. Wesley and Whitefield did agree on one vital point: their duty to win souls to Jesus Christ. In later years, with more wisdom and probably more meekness, these two men achieved a measure of reconciliation. Whitefield, in October 1741, penned a personal letter to Wesley:

> Though much may be said for my doing it, yet I am sorry now that any such thing dropped from my pen and I humbly ask pardon. I find I love you as much as ever and pray God, if it be his blessed will, that we be all united together . . . May God remove all obstacles that now prevent our union! . . . In about three weeks I hope to be in Bristol. May all disputings cease, and each of us talk of nothing but Jesus and him crucified. This is my resolution.[17]

A couple of months later the two men met in Bristol. In the meantime, Whitefield had married Elizabeth Delamotte, who happened to be a friend of John Wesley. (Isn't it interesting how God works to achieve reconciliation!) When the two men met, George recognized his responsibility for the breakup of fellowship and they agreed to love one another, even though they would continue to work separately. Seven years later, Wesley recorded his rejoicing in the way that God had used Whitefield and also commented after hearing him preach, "How wise is God in giving different talents to different preachers!"[18] While it was not always so among his followers, Wesley never encouraged criticism of Whitefield. One small-minded disciple once asked, "Do you think we shall see Mr. Whitefield in heaven?" "No," Wesley replied, and the man looked pleased that he had aimed his flattery well. "No sir," said Wesley, "I fear not. Mr. Whitefield will be so near the Throne and we at such a distance we shall hardly get a sight of him."[19]

3. We can agree to cooperate as the Spirit leads.

Wesley and Whitefield agreed to love one another as brothers, but this spirit of unity did not mean they worked together. They did agree on one point: the need to win souls to Christ. Sometimes our differences as Christians will be so striking that it will be difficult to work closely with each other. However, different groups can still respect each other as joint-heirs with Christ, and cooperate in some situations. In our city, over fifty churches, with little fellowship and many differences, have cooperated in several evangelistic efforts which have been very fruitful. Stephen Clark calls this "cooperative ecumenism":

> Cooperative ecumenism proceeds on the presupposition that Christians of various traditions do not have full agreement or unity, and we do not expect it for some time to come. In the meantime, however, we acknowledge the requirement that we should love one another as brothers and sisters, looking forward to the time when the Lord will make greater unity possible. We will cooperate wherever and whenever we can make Christ known and strengthen those who follow him. Our rule is that we will try to do whatever builds up. Sometimes the rule indicates not cooperating in

certain ways, though we might personally be inclined to do so, because of the need to take into account others in our churches who do not see things our way and to avoid worsening relations between churches. Nonetheless, the spirit behind cooperative ecumenism urges us to lay down our lives for all those whom we recognize as true brothers and sisters in Christ, and with them to advance the cause of Christ.[20]

E. Stanley Jones said the same thing in a concise manner:

Here we enter a fellowship;
Sometimes we will agree to differ;
Always we will resolve to love
And unite to serve.[21]

In Jesus, our common denominators are greater than our differences. In Him our commonality is eternal and must be emphasized. Our differences are temporal and must be subordinated for the sake of unity.

Love is Our Priority

Love is our priority: *above all these things put on love.*[22] One of my favorite biblical prayers is *that God through His Spirit would grant that we, being rooted and established in love, may have power, together with all the saints, to grasp how wide and long and high and deep is the love of Christ.*[23] We close this chapter with three additional quotes by three great leaders which should challenge every Christian:

We are to love all true Christian brothers in a way that the world may observe. This means showing love to our brothers in the midst of our differences – great or

155

small – loving our brothers when it costs us something, loving them even under times of tremendous emotional tension, loving them in a way the world can see. In short, we are to practice and exhibit the holiness of God and the love of God, for without this we can grieve the Holy Spirit.

Love – and the unity it attests to – is the mark Christ gave Christians to wear before the world. Only with this mark may the world know that Christians are indeed Christians and that Jesus was sent by the Father.[24]

Francis Schaeffer

The only way any Church can get a blessing is to lay aside all difference, all criticism, all coldness and party feeling, and come to the Lord as one man; and when the Church lives in the power of the 13th chapter of First Corinthians I am sure that many will be added daily to the flock of God.[25]

D. L. Moody

I sometimes dream of a church healed in love, no longer divided into armed camps, but caring passionately about winning others to Christ and striving for the righteousness of God's justice. We have not yet seen what that kind of whole church will do for the needs of this fragmented world.[26]

Charles Colson

Chapter Fourteen
The Church in the City

In Scripture we see a wonderful sense of unity and interaction among various, local congregations. Local churches in New Testament times did not have the various names we give churches. They were simply called, for example, "the church in Jerusalem" or "the church in Antioch." The city seems to be the basic dimension of unity recorded in Scripture. Paul never talks of the "churches" at Corinth, but the "church" at Corinth.[1] In Revelation, the apostle John addresses believers in seven cities, but only one church in each city is mentioned:

- *The church in Ephesus* (2:1)
- *The church in Smyrna* (2:8)
- *The church in Pergamum* (2:12)
- *The church in Thyatira* (2:18)
- *The church in Sardis* (3:1)
- *The church in Philadelphia* (3:7)
- *The church in Laodicea* (3:14)

The New Testament authors saw the church in each city as one unit. With an estimated 10,000-50,000 believers in some of those cities, the believers did not have the same meeting places and the same leaders; yet they saw themselves as one. As in local congregations today, they sometimes had problems with quarrels

157

or division over leadership.[2] Yet in the Lord's perspective each particular city had only one church. In the Bible we see the word "church" used in the singular in regard to believers in a specific city. With one exception,[3] the plural form churches is used when referring to a larger geographical region– e.g., *the churches of Judea*[4] or *the churches of Asia*.[5] J. N. Darby rightly taught,

> The Church originally was an assemblage of all believers in any given locality . . . he who was not a member of the Church in the place in which he dwelt, was no member of Christ's Church at all . . .[6]

In our cities, we see a lot of congregations, but the Lord sees the big picture – ONE CHURCH. This "one city–one church" concept is seen in several scriptural analogies:

• Our churches are like many individual lights, but together we are *a* lighted city. In a verse that we usually interpret in an individual sense, Jesus said, *You [plural] are the light . . . a city . . .*[7] A single light can be put under a bushel, but a city – the corporate light – is set on a hill and can not be hidden. This lighted city is the light of the world and cannot escape notice.[8]

• Our churches are like many separate structures, but together we make *one* temple building. The temple in Jesus' day consisted of many buildings which was referred to as one temple building.[9] Scripture says that *all the buildings* are being fitted together and growing into a singular *holy temple in the Lord.*[10]

• Our churches are like many different components of *one* golden lampstand. In the book of Revelation, seven city churches are compared to *seven lampstands.*[11]

In each city there will normally be many assemblies, yet one lampstand. In the tabernacle design we see a description of the lampstand: *They made the lampstand of pure gold and hammered it out, base and shaft; its flowerlike cups, buds and blossoms were of one piece with it.*[12] There were seven branches, various cups, buds, and blossoms, and other components in this intricate artwork; yet there was a unity – all the components were ultimately one.

The church in a city is like many components which make one lampstand.

It is interesting that in Scripture no other name but the name of a locality is ever connected with a church. This does not mean we necessarily discard all of our church names. As individual congregations, we can maintain individuality and distinct characteristics, yet recognize that we are working to build the church in the city.

We Need to See the Larger Picture

We need to see the larger picture of the body of Christ in a city – varied assemblies, but one church. Do we have a burden to see the Lord bless other congregations in our city? Do we view other believers on the other side of town as brothers, or as "half-brothers?" Do we rejoice when another church experiences revival and growth or do we harbor secret envy? Are we willing to be an instrument to help bridge the gap?

Our individual congregations are not an end to themselves, but a part of something much larger that God is forming. When new folks inquire about our congregation, I frequently mention that we appreciate other congregations who honor Christ and that we are not in competition with other members of the body. Each of us has different pieces of the grand puzzle that God alone is putting together. Each congregation may have some unique contributions, but none of us has the complete package; each of us is only an individual part of the entire work of God.

Each congregation has unique pieces, but no one congregation has the whole puzzle!

In a city we may not be able to "get all the churches together," but we can connect with a piece close to us. In some cities, there are interdenominational movements going on which are profitable for the body of Christ. In our area we participate in a once-a- month fellowship group for pastors from a variety of backgrounds. Some leaders from various congregations cooperate in a limited form of unity – e.g., Baptists may work together with other Baptist churches, Pentecostal assemblies may fellowship with other Pentecostal assemblies, or some of us may enjoy relationships with a few other groups who "think the way we do." Although this kind of cooperation does express a measure of unity, it falls short of a much broader dimension of the city-wide unity that God intends.

In major cities, any unity which is worked out in a practical expression will probably be in a regional sense. In large cities it would be almost impossible to bring the entire Christian population together in one place. In New York City, for example, even Yankee Stadium would not hold all the believers if they came together. We can seek cooperation with other evangelical churches who are geographically close to us, yet still recognize one church in the city.

Recognizing the Body of Christ

Now there are many members, but one body.[13]

In a pastors' gathering a simple, but profound prophetic word came forth about unity in the church: "It's not organizing; it's not compromising; it's RECOGNIZING the Body of Christ." We may not see it, but in God's perspective the church in our locality is already one. Roland Allen, in his classic, *Missionary Methods, St. Paul's or Ours?* pointed out:

> St. Paul began with unity. In his view the unity of the Church was not something to be created, but something which already existed and was to be maintained. Churches were not independent unities: they were extensions of an already existing unity. There could be no such thing as two churches in the same place both holding the Head, yet not in communion with one another. There could be no such thing as a Christian

baptized into Christ Jesus not in communion with all the other members of the body of which Christ was the Head. If a member was united to the Head he was united to all the other members.

There was a spiritual unity in the one Lord, the one faith, the one baptism, the one God and Father of all. There was no such thing as spiritual unity expressed in outward separation.[14]

When we unite with Christ, we unite with all others who have chosen to follow Him. Andrew Murray, the Dutch Reformed pastor and author of books on the deeper life, expressed the need to recognize a unity that already exists in the spiritual realm:

Believers ARE ONE. They have not made nor can they unmake the unity. It is ours to RECOGNIZE it and act upon it as one of God's facts. Recognize the unity.[15]

Murray not only taught this concept of unity, but exemplified his teaching in practice. In his hospitable home at Wellington, South Africa, ministers and members of any church which acknowledged Jesus as Savior and Head were "cordially welcomed as brethren beloved, and made to feel immediately at home."[16]

We should seek a greater view of the church as a whole, to see the body of Christ as it is. So often when there is talk of "the church" or "praying for revival" or "saving souls," we only think about our own little assembly. Suppose our group has been praying fervently over months for revival and then one day we hear of many getting saved in another assembly across town? Do we rejoice? Or, are we jealous? We need not ever be jealous of other believers, because we belong to each other!

For all things belong to you, whether Paul or Apollos or Cephas—all things belong to you.[17]

This is a truth we must grasp – IT ALL BELONGS TO US! If a pastor across town is having great success, I do not need to be envious; his success is part of me! What is happening at his church belongs to our church! In the physical body, my fingers do not resent my toes; they function differently, but the fingers appreciate the toes! Likewise, each of us is unique, and yet we belong to each other. Because we are all part of the same body, we are *mutually dependent on one another*.[18] We can appreciate every "toe," "kidney," and "eye" in the body of Christ.

> *And some of the parts that seem weakest and least important are really the most necessary. Yes, we are especially glad to have some parts that seem rather odd!*[19]

If a part of our body is weak or even sick, then every joint feels it and the body will suffer until that part regains health. This is why we should pray for the entire body of Christ in our community. None of us can individually achieve the fullness that God intends without each other. He works *until we all reach unity in the faith . . . and become mature, attaining to the whole measure of the fullness of Christ.*[20]

Do we appreciate the larger body of Christ? We must lift our eyes to see the church not as *our* group, but as *the* church of the Lord Jesus Christ, consisting of every born-again believer, regardless of whether he worships in the Baptist, Presbyterian, or Pentecostal church. We may see a church in our city that appears to be divided, immature, and lacking in many regards. We might know pastors or members obsessed with building their own churches and ignoring Christians in other congregations. We should not be discouraged. The Lord is building His church in our city as he is throughout the world, and He is more interested in this work than we are! We should commit ourselves to a local expression of His body, even if the other members do not share this vision for the church. We can refuse to compromise our convictions and yet be loving and forbearing to our brethren.

We can conduct ourselves within a local church *as though the church were one.*

Leaders are Essential for Church Unity

Behold, how good and how pleasant it is for brothers to dwell together in unity! It is like the precious oil upon the head, coming down upon the beard, even Aaron's beard, coming down upon the edge of his robes. It is like the dew of Hermon coming down upon the mountains of Zion; for there the Lord commanded the blessing – life forever.[21]

Like the oil flowing down from the head, unity flows downward. Although it is essential for all members to pursue unity, if leaders are uninterested or haphazard about unity, generally little will happen. This psalm promises both an anointing of His Spirit [*the precious oil poured on*] and a heavenly refreshing [*the dew of Hermon . . . falling*] for Christians gathered in unity. This promise should especially be relevant to leaders who desire God's fullest blessing on their life and work. Leaders should be the pacesetters in building unity, not unnecessary competitors, as Frank Damazio has exhorted:

The problem of church divisions is rampant today not primarily because the congregational members are unwilling to unite with other Christians; but, rather, because the church leaders are so busy competing with one another in the expansion of their own little kingdoms, that unity is a threat unless their leaders are first united. The cry and need of the Church is for unity among its leaders as an example for the people to follow.[22]

In our day, God is calling leaders together. Not all will respond to His call, but some will. What is needed initially is not more structured "ministerial associations," but informal fellowship in small groups – two, three, or four leaders coming together. For some pastors who are used to formal, religious meetings, the idea of simply coming together for fellowship and relating as friends in Christ may be somewhat threatening. It may be difficult for some leaders to share openly and honestly with other men about what is happening in their lives, families, and churches.

Do we as leaders take initiative to get together with other leaders on a one-to-one basis for informal fellowship? Richard Baxter, in his classic work, *The Reformed Pastor*, encouraged this mutual interaction among leaders:

> My last request is, that all the faithful ministers of Christ would, without any more delay, unite and associate for the furtherance of each other in the work of the Lord, and the maintaining of unity and concord in his churches. And that they would not neglect their brotherly meetings to those ends . . .[23]

If leaders in our communities fail to take initiative to fellowship and be genuinely interested in other leaders, it is unlikely our area will see the kind of unity for which Jesus prayed. It must begin with leaders who are willing to die to self and see the larger perspective of God's kingdom around them.

Ministerial organizations may be a natural outcome of informal fellowship together, but unless relationships have been built first we will have the "cart before the horse" and may have one more lifeless organization. Relationships in the kingdom of God will take time and commitment, but it will be worth the effort. There is a special anointing and blessing from God that is awaiting the body of Christ when leaders come together in unity.

A Realistic View of Unity

We must realize not all pastors or believers will be interested in relating with different groups of Christians, but this fact should not hinder God's work of unity. One of the best pictures of unity in the Bible is found in II Chronicles 30. This was a divided time in Israel's history – the nation was split with Judah in the south and Israel in the north. There was much division and strife among the tribes. King Hezekiah was one of Israel's better kings. In the wisdom of God, he invited *all* the tribes to come together to celebrate the Passover, which had been neglected for many years. This in itself is symbolic – communion, celebration of our Passover Lamb [Jesus], can be a focal point in bringing us together. The emphasis was on the Passover, not on their differences. As the invitations were sent out, notice the response:

> *Now Hezekiah sent to all Israel and Judah and wrote letters also to Ephraim and Manasseh, that they should come to the house of the Lord at Jerusalem to celebrate the Passover of the Lord God of Israel . . .*
>
> *So the courier passed from city to city through the country of Ephraim and Manasseh, and as far as Zebulun, but they laughed them to scorn, and mocked them. Nevertheless some men of Asher, Manasseh, and Zebulun humbled themselves and came to Jerusalem. The hand of God was also on Judah to give them one heart to do what the king and the princes commanded by the word of the Lord.*[24]

Not everyone came together in unity. Judah was united in coming together, but Israel had a twofold response: some laughed, mocked, and stayed home, while others made the trip. The same is true today–not everyone sees a need for unity, and because of this, some may miss out on the blessed results of unity. The Lord is not going to "twist our arms" to bring us together. Not every pastor or every believer will be interested in unity or in recognizing the body of Christ. Those who are willing to come together, however, will receive a blessing. For two consecutive years we invited all the churches in our county to cancel Sunday morning meetings on a particular date and come together at a large, centrally located exposition hall for a joint assembly meeting of praise and preaching. Over thirty churches came together while many others decided not to attend. For those who came together, it was a tremendous blessing and enlarged our hearts toward one another. We did not fret over those who did not attend. Notice the great blessing in our story of the various tribes gathering for the Passover gathering:

> *And sons of Israel present in Jerusalem celebrated the Feast of Unleavened Bread for seven days with great joy, and the Levites and the priest praised the Lord day after day with loud instruments to the Lord. Then Hezekiah spoke encouragingly to all the Levites who showed good insight in the things of the Lord. So they ate for the appointed seven days, sacrificing peace offerings and giving thanks to the Lord God of their fathers. Then the whole assembly decided to celebrate the feast another seven days, so they celebrated the seven days with joy.* [25]

What a tremendous celebration! Not only did God's people enjoy the required seven day feast, but they decided to fellowship another seven days! There was no "arm twisting" going on here – only joy, praise, and encouragement! Lord, may we see more of this in our own communities!

Working Together in the Harvest

In many regions of the country, God has linked congregations from various cities in His Spirit to build relationships, share teaching, stand against works of darkness, assist in church problems, and work together in the harvest. We see this translocal emphasis in Scripture: Paul asked that his letter to the brethren in Colossae be shared with the brethren in Laodicea.[26] He told the Thessalonians to be imitators of the churches of God who were in Judea.[27] We have the record of the Corinthian church giving financially to the church in Jerusalem.[28] Because of modern travel, believers can easily drive miles to participate in fellowship. Therefore, church unity sometimes extends throughout a region or between cities. Such associations will usually be more relational than organizational – brothers interacting with brothers as the need arises and the Spirit leads.

As we think of "one church in the city," it does not mean we all have to think alike or meet at the same place. Peter Wagner clarified this concept,

> The church of the city . . . does not necessarily mean structural unity or the existence of a local "superchurch." Nor does it imply that all denominations are to be abolished. The emphasis is rather on one church, made up of diverse congregations with their respective traditions, convictions, shades and characteristics, but working together to further the same mission, share resources and leadership, and join forces to combat the enemy.[29]

Wagner also has pointed out an excellent example in God's work among the churches in Argentina. In that nation, there are Pastoral Councils, or presbyteries, in various cities where the leaders recognize there is only one church in the city. Wagner reported,

> The creation of the Pastoral Councils in the majority of the cities of Argentina is a marvelous work of the Holy Spirit. At present there exist more than 200 Pastoral

Councils throughout the nation, and several more are added every year. The remarkable orientation toward unity in the church leadership is not the result of one person's vision, nor is it the work of a committee. Quite spontaneously, by the work of the Holy Spirit, these councils have been emerging independently in the cities and towns of Argentina. . . .

The pastoral Councils . . . help the local congregations enjoy the diversity and richness of the whole Body of Christ. Congregations are encouraged to share the multiplicity of resources with which God has blessed the church in the city. . . . The Council prays and stands in the breach, interceding for the city and people. . . . And, above all, it seeks God's vision for the city as a whole and develops a missionary strategy common to all, truly impacting the city with the gospel of Jesus Christ.[30]

We may have our differences in our various churches, but we can come together in the work of the kingdom; we are exhorted by Scripture to be *contending as one man for the faith of the gospel.*[31] This gospel story illustrates this point:

> *Simon answered, "Master, we've worked hard all night and haven't caught anything. But because you say so, I will let down the nets."*
>
> *When they had done so, they caught such a large number of fish that their nets began to break. So they signaled their partners in the other boat to come and help them, and they came and filled both boats so full that they began to sink.*[32]

In this passage two different boats – each doing their own fishing – came together for one great catch. These various boats did not simply have meetings to discuss unity; *they came together in the work.* Conferences about unity have their place, but greater unity will likely be seen as we work together.

The various tribes of Israel were often united in their work, as they were when they rebuilt the walls of Jerusalem.[33] They were also united in their warfare: *All the men of Israel were gathered against the city, united as one man.*[34]

In our own county, we have had a difficult time getting pastors together for regular fellowship. However, we have had three joint evangelistic outreaches in which thirty to fifty churches participated. These outreaches were not only very successful, but they also drew various leaders together who had no interaction up to that point.

As the church unites in spiritual warfare against the forces of darkness, we will see unity naturally taking place. In many cities, believers have come together to stand against abortion, pornography, and other forms of ungodliness. There is cooperation and fellowship taking place in this regard between believers of varied backgrounds. Scripture prophetically declares that one day believers will *serve Him shoulder to shoulder.*[35]

May God give us eyes to see His church as one body in a greater way; and, may He link us together with other brethren as He sees fit.

Chapter Fifteen

God's Glorious Church: The Bride of Christ

Christ also loved the church and gave Himself up for her . . . that He might present to Himself the church in all her glory, having no spot or wrinkle or any such thing; but that she would be holy and blameless.[1]

The love Christ has for his bride – his true followers – is incredible, beyond our comprehension. In referring to the king, the Song of Songs mentions *the day of his wedding, the day his heart rejoiced.*[2] I can remember the day of my wedding as I stepped into the front of a church and soon looked up at the end of the center aisle as my beautiful, smiling bride began to make her way slowly toward me. My heart was racing a mile-a-minute! I felt like leaping and shouting! The joy was incredible! Being united to this woman in marriage was the happiest day of my life! Some of you may have equally enjoyed such a delightful experience. Knowing such human responses, can we imagine our Lord Jesus actually *rejoicing* – being extremely thrilled about his bride?

For all eternity, the Heavenly Father has had one glorious climax in mind – He has been preparing a Bride who will one day be united with her heavenly Bridegroom. The grandest event in all the universe will occur when the Lord Jesus comes again, resurrects our mortal bodies into immortal ones, takes his people to himself, looks upon us face-to-face, and invites us into the Marriage Supper of the Lamb. This will be God the Father's final product, the completion of all his purposes, the consummation of the ages. Paul Billheimer discussed this divine grand finale.

> The final and ultimate outcome and goal of events from eternity to eternity, the finished product of all the ages, is the spotless Bride of Christ, united with Him in wedded bliss at the Marriage Supper of the Lamb and seated with her heavenly Bridegroom upon the throne of the universe – ruling and reigning with Him over an ever increasing and expanding Kingdom. He entered the stream of human history for this one purpose, to claim His Beloved (Rev. 19:6, 9; 21:7, 9, 10).
>
> *Thus the Church, and only the Church, is the key to and explanation of history.* The Church, blood-washed and spotless, is the center, the reason, and the goal of all of God's vast creative handiwork. Therefore, history is only the handmaiden of the Church, and the nations of the world are but puppets manipulated by God for the purposes of His Church (Acts 17:26). *Creation has no other aim. History has no other goal.* From before the foundation of the world until the dawn of eternal ages God has been working toward one grand event, one supreme end – the glorious wedding of His Son, the Marriage Supper of the Lamb.[3]

Should We Expect to See a Perfected Church Before Our Lord Returns?

Some Bible teachers imply that before Christ comes again we will see a great harvest of souls, unparalleled in church history. The church will finally be perfected, walking in all of New Testament truth and power, a *glorious church without any spots or wrinkles*. As good as this sounds, however, what do the Scriptures really say about a *glorious church?*

We may very well see some amazing things in His body before the Lord returns. Indeed, in some parts of the world, like communist China, incredible works of God are currently taking place. Believers, in general, have an expectation that the best is yet to come! Scripture says, *The whole creation is on tiptoe to see the wonderful sight of the sons of God coming into their own.*[4]

However, on this earth we should not anticipate a perfect church. Some believers go through life quite unhappy because the church never seems to reach a perfection they think was in the New Testament church, or that they think will be in the end-time church. For some people, a perfected church on earth is what captivates their thoughts and motivates their action (or lack of action). But, Scripture simply does not suggest that we will experience a perfect church in this lifetime. Whom do we expect to be included in the Lord's glorious church that will have no spots or wrinkles? Is it only that small fraction of the church throughout the years of human history that happen to be alive at the time of his coming? No, rather the Marriage Supper of the Lamb will include millions of believers who died throughout the centuries and yet never attained perfection on this earth. Why should we assume that we will see a perfected body of believers on the earth in one particular generation? We can certainly expect to see a measure of restoration in the church of the last days, but Scripture makes it clear that it will only be when He appears, *we shall be like Him, for we shall see Him as He is.*[5] We can take heart in this fact– all the imperfections of our personal life and corporate church life *will* be changed – at the sound of the Lord's final trumpet.[6]

We Have a Connection with the Church of All Ages

Therefore, since we are surrounded by such a great cloud of witnesses, let us throw off everything that hinders and the sin that so easily entangles, and let us run with perseverance the race marked out for us.[7]

But you have come to Mount Zion, to the heavenly Jerusalem, the city of the living God. You have come to thousands upon thousands of angels in joyful assembly, to the church of the firstborn, whose names are written in heaven. You have come to God, the judge of all men, to the spirits of righteous men made perfect, to Jesus the mediator of a new covenant, and to the sprinkled blood that speaks a better word than the blood of Abel.[8]

The Scripture says we *have come* to the *heavenly Jerusalem*. In a mysterious way we are currently connected with the believers who have gone on before us. We must clarify, however, that there is no biblical indication we should ever pray to departed saints, and trying to communicate with the dead is strictly forbidden in Scripture.[9] So, we do not need to be overly mystical about this connection, but simply appreciate that great multitude of saints who have led the way for us – the early apostles, the reformers, missionary pioneers, and lesser known believers. God is not just interested in an end-time church; He has always been deeply interested in His bride – the church of all the ages. This is the church Charles Wesley wrote about in his hymn, "Come, Let Us Join Our Friends Above."

One family we dwell in him,
    One Church, above, beneath,
Though now divided by the stream,
    The narrow stream of death:

174

One army of the living God,
    To His command we bow;
Part of his host have crossed the flood,
    And part are crossing now.

Whenever I watch a church history film about Wycliffe, Huss, Wesley, Luther, etc., my eyes often fill with tears. I find a greater appreciation for our brethren who often paid a personal price for what we contemporary Christians currently enjoy, and I also feel a greater connection with this "fellowship of the saints."

How Perfected was the Early Church?

Most modern day churches fall short of the high standard of maturity and holiness found in the New Testament examples. However, these New Testament church bodies themselves were far from perfect. Some Galatian believers had been taken in by serious doctrinal errors. Some disciples in Thessalonica had permitted "last days" thinking to cause many of them to fall into sinful idleness. The Corinthians probably had the most problems; they were a company of born-again believers, quite gifted by the Holy Spirit, and yet we find in their midst divisions, factions, lawsuits, immorality, and even drunkenness at the Lord's table! The apostle Paul addressed these issues directly, yet he displayed no intolerant attitude nor threw up his hands in disgust at their imperfection. He begins his letter by saying, *"I always thank God for you because of His grace given you in Christ Jesus. For in him you have been enriched in every way . . ."*[10] The apostle Paul held out some high standards, but he also could live and work humbly with God's people just where they were.

Scripture indicates there will be a mixture in the church up to the end. There will be tares among the wheat; there will be goats among the sheep; there will be a Judas among the disciples. The Westminster Confession of Faith stated, "The purest churches under heaven are subject both to mixture and error . . ."[11]

Lance Lambert offered words of wisdom for those pursuing the "perfect church:"

We have this idea amongst Christian people that the church – the true church – is perfect, and this is what we're looking for. We're looking for a perfect company. But my dear friends, if you find a perfect company of God's children, you have not found the church. You have found a little, exclusive, elitist group, but you have not found the church. Let me prove this to you very simply. Let's suppose we have a marvelous little group, about 30-40 strong. We've weeded out all the hopeless ones, kicked them out, sent them off to the other places, and we have gone deeper and deeper so that those who couldn't understand have finally gone away to other assemblies, and here we are – the 30-35 of us. We are the ongoing overcomers. At last, we are an overcomer company.

Now we have a prayer meeting, and in our prayer meeting we take hold of the Lord and someone who's just been saved (and we've got our suspicions about him anyway) gets up in our premises: "Lord! We're so burdened for unsaved people. Save them, Lord!" And guess what happens? The Spirit of God falls upon our locality and overnight 500 people are saved, and they all come to our meeting! Now we're 535 in number! But the most terrible thing has happened – we've got drunkards, alcoholics, pimps, prostitutes, the immoral, those who have AIDS, and a whole number of other things; not all of them – thank God, we say, there are at least 200 that are normal – but everybody else, what are we going to do with them!? Our perfect church is no longer perfect! Why is this so? Because it is a real church, that's why. Suddenly we have all the problems that a true church should have. This is so because the true church is a melting pot, a kind of cutting out room, a workshop. It is the place where the Holy Spirit transforms sinners by His grace.[12]

We Are God's Workmanship

For we are God's workmanship, created in Christ Jesus to do good works, which God prepared in advance for us to do.[13]

The church is God's project. We are *God's workmanship*, not the work of a man. The Phillips translation says it well: *The fact that what we are we owe to the hand of God upon us.*

The church is also in a process. The Greek tense implies that we are *continually* his workmanship. We are a house under construction, eventually to become what the Designer has in mind. And *in him you, too, are being built together to become a dwelling in which God lives by his Spirit.*[14] When we see construction of a house in the beginning stages, we notice all the exposed wood, gaping holes, unfinished siding, and debris scattered everywhere. In the eyes of the architect, however, the final product is envisioned. The same is true with God, the master architect of the glorious church. Since God is not restricted to time, he looks upon us as a work in process, but he also sees HIS FINISHED PRODUCT!

- We see all the imperfections and immaturity.
  God sees us *complete in Christ.*[15]
- We see all the sin and compromise.
  God sees us as *righteous in Christ.*[16]
- We see all our deficiencies and inadequacies.
  God sees us having *everything we need for life and godliness.*[17]

DURING CONSTRUCTION, WE SEE ALL THE MESS; THE MASTER ARCHITECT SEES THE FINISHED PRODUCT!

The church is the very best God can do. Instead of *God's workmanship* in Eph. 2:10, the Jerusalem Bible says, *We are God's work of art*. The New Living Translation says, *We are God's masterpiece*. We are not just an ordinary piece of carpentry, some cheap painting, or some shanty house; we are the very best the Master can do! As God describes his people in the Old Testament, he often calls them *Zion, the city of God*. Notice what he says:

> *Glorious things are said of you,*
> *O city of God . . .*[18]
> *Out of Zion, the perfection of beauty,*
> *God has shone forth.*[19]

Amazing – despite all our flaws and failings, God calls us *glorious* and *the perfection of beauty*! In the first few chapters of the book of Revelation, we see seven churches and all the problems they have. Yet, the Lord calls them his *golden lampstands* and He is said to be *walking among them.*[20] Even with all their flaws, the churches are *lampstands*. Shining forth the light of Jesus, they are described as *golden*, representing the highest quality. God has no contingency plan for his church if it fails; it is his very best workmanship, and God Himself – through the Holy Spirit – will make sure the work gets finished. Watchman Nee made these comments on "God's workmanship:"

> We are his workmanship. . . . The church is the very best God can produce. It can never be improved upon. We look around and see breakdown everywhere and we wonder, "Where is the Church coming to?" I tell you, she is not "coming to" anything; she has arrived. We do not look forward to discover her goal; we look back. God reached His end in Christ before the foundation of the world, and we move forward with him on the basis of what already is. As we move in the light of that eternal fact, we witness its progressive manifestation. . . .
>
> We need to revise our thinking about the Church. It is not an organization to be planned, nor is it a company of people to be completed. It is not a concept to be grasped, nor an ideal to be attained. Like so much else that is ours in Christ, the Church is a reality to be seen with the help of the Holy Spirit through the Word . . . and once the Lord has begun to open our eyes, we no longer despise small things. We no longer say, when we meet only a handful of believers in some place, "Of what use is this to God? There are so few here!" We do not complain, "There is only one other brother with me in this pagan city!"
>
> The implications of all this are very great. We have no business to view things materialistically or

179

intellectually – that is, through the eyes of Rome or of the Reformation – but only from the standpoint of God. God sees "seven golden lampstands." He knows only "the Church", and when we permit the Spirit of truth to lead us into the spiritual truth of the Church, we shall see only the Church that God sees.[21]

Therefore, every believer ought to invest time, energy, and money in the church of Jesus Christ! We could invest in no earthly institution and have assurance that it would never fail. But, our Lord Jesus has shed his blood to ensure that his project will be completed: *I will build my church, and the gates of Hades will not overcome it.*[22]

A London newspaper once offered a prize for the best essay on the subject: "What is wrong with the church?" The prize was won by a minister from Wales. He gave the answer: "What is wrong with the church is our failure to realize and wonder at the beauty, the mystery, the glory, and the greatness of the church."[23]

So, as we see all the human flaws in the church and even at times are tempted to despair, do not lose hope! God the Father sees things differently. Jesus, God's Son, has shed his blood and paid for our redemption. The Holy Spirit has been sent to build his church, to prepare his glorious bride, and to finish the Father's wonderful artistic work – his church – that we see in the process. Saints of God, let us rejoice and be quite optimistic about the future of the church – we are God's very best; we are his workmanship!

INTRODUCTION NOTES: ON WHAT FOUNDATION ARE WE BUILDING?

1. Story told by DeVern Fromke to our fellowship, and recounted in two written versions: Message on "The Judgment Seat of Christ" in *Rivers of Living Water* magazine, Winter 2005 (Encinitas, CA) and in a shorter form in Fromke's book, *No Other Foundation* (Sure Foundation, Indianapolis, IN, 1965), pp. 35-36.

2. I Cor. 3:10-15

3. Fromke, op. cit.

4. Fromke, op. cit.

5. I Sam. 16:7

6. I Cor. 4:5

7. Charles Farah, *From the Pinnacle of the Temple* (Logos International, Plainfield, NJ), p. 207

8. Rom. 14:5

9. Matt 13:52

10. Several older works of mine – because I am now revising them – will likely not be reprinted. These include *God is Bringing Animals of Every Kind into the Ark; Myths of the Ministry;* and *Little Foxes That Ruin the Vineyard.*

11. *Decision* magazine, April 1993 issue (Billy Graham Evangelistic Assoc., Charlotte, NC)

12. 1 Thes. 5:21

CHAPTER ONE NOTES: THE CHURCH IS THE DWELLING PLACE OF GOD

1. John 1:14 NAS

2. Lev. 26:11-12 NAS

3. Eph. 3:17 translation by Kenneth Wuest, *The New Testament: An Expanded Translation* (Eerdmans, Grand Rapids, MI, 1961)

4. Ps. 132:13

5. Eph. 2:22

6. Rev. 21:3

7. John 1:38

8. Ps. 132:4-5

9. Harry Verploegh, *A.W. Tozer: An Anthology* (Christian Publications, Camp Hill, PA, 1984), p. 60

10. Charles Colson, *Presenting Belief in an Age of Unbelief* (Victor Books, Wheaton, IL, 1986), p. 35

11. Stuart Briscoe, *All Things Weird and Wonderful* (Victor Books, Wheaton, IL, 1977), p. 47

12. I Pet. 2:9 NAS

CHAPTER TWO NOTES: THE CHURCH IS A FAMILY, NOT A GROCERY STORE

1. W. J. Ern Baxter, *The Chief Shepherd and His Sheep* (Timothy Publishing Co., Spring Valley, CA, 1987), p. 56

2. Eph. 2:19 NLT

3. Ps. 68:6

4. Heb. 2:11

5. I Pet. 2:17

6. Rom. 8:29 Revised English Bible

7. Acts 2:42

8. Fenelon, *Let Go* (Whitaker House, Springdale, PA, 1973,) pp. 43, 50

9. Stuart Briscoe, *Purifying the Church* (Regal Books, Ventura, CA, 1987), p. 106

10. I Cor. 12:21-25

11. I Cor. 12:21

12. II Cor. 10:7 New Jerusalem Bible

13. Lk. 18:11

14. Watchman Nee, *The Character of God's Workman* (Christian Fellowship Publishers, New York, 1988), p. 34

15. Rom. 14:4,10 Phillips

16. We see this term in all seven churches portrayed in Revelation (Rev. 2:7, 11, 17, 26; 3:4, 12, 21)

17. Ex. 34:29

18. Rom. 12:16 Phillips

19. David McCasland, *Oswald Chambers: Abandoned to God* (Discovery House Publishers, Nashville, TN, 1993,) p. 157

20. Fenelon, Let Go (Whitaker House, Springdale, PA, 1973), p. 50

21. Rom. 15:1

22. Derek Prince, *New Wine Magazine,* Nov. 1977 (Mobile, AL)

23. I Pet. 2:9 NAS

24. Robert Girard, *Brethren Hang Loose* (Zondervan Publishing House, Grand Rapids, MI), p. 123

25. John Wimber, article in *Equipping the Saints* magazine (Anaheim, CA), Summer 1993 issue

26. Bill Hull, *Building High Commitment in a Low-Commitment World* (Fleming Revell, Grand Rapids, MI, 1995), pp. 18-19

CHAPTER THREE NOTES: THE CHURCH IS AN EQUIPPING CENTER, NOT A SYMPATHY CLUB

1. William Barclay, *New Testament Words* (SCM Press Ltd., London, England, 1964), pp. 220-221

2. John Miller, *Outgrowing the Ingrown Church* (Zondervan Publishing Co., Grand Rapids, MI, 1986), p. 20

3. Rom. 14:1

4. Rom. 8:28-29

5. Eph. 4:12

6. II Tim. 2:3

7. Jean Vanier, quoted in Ralph Neighbour, *Where Do We Go From Here?* (Touch Publications, Houston, TX, 1990), p. 113

8. Mk. 8:34

9. Matt. 22:36-37

10. Prov. 18:2

11. Phil. 2:4

12. Larry Crabb, *Men and Women* (Zondervan Publishing House, Grand Rapids, MI, 1991), pp. 53, 76-77

13. Matt. 6:33

14. I Tim. 5:4-10

15. Dietrich Bonhoeffer, *Life Together,* translated by John Doberstein (Harper and Row Publishers, New York, NY, 1965), p. 76

16. Joseph Stowell, *Shepherding the Church* (Moody Press, Chicago, 1994, 1997), pp. 197-198

17. II Kings 6:27

18. Ps. 62:5-6

19. A.B. Simpson, "The Church in the Heavenlies," published in *The Best of A.B. Simpson*, compiled by Keith Bailey (Christian Publications, Camp Hill, PA, 1987), p. 99

20. R. J. Rushdoony, *Chalcedon Report*, May 1981 (P.O. Box 158, Vallecito, CA)

CHAPTER FOUR: THE CHURCH IS THE PILLAR AND SUPPORT OF THE TRUTH

1. I Tim. 3:15

2. Greek *hedraioma*. See Bauer, Arndt, and Gingrich, *A Greek-English Lexicon of the New Testament* (The University of Chicago Press, Chicago, 1957) and Henry Thayer (on the verb form of the word, hedraioo), *Thayer's Greek-English Lexicon of the New Testament* (Associated Publishers, Grand Rapids, MI)

3. Greek *stulos*, op. cit.

4. James Garrett, paper "The New Testament Church and Heresy," p. 17. This excellent paper and others may be obtained from the internet. Check jim@doulospress.org or write to Doulos Press, PO Box 50130, Tulsa, OK 74150-0130

5. W. Robertson Nicoll, *The Expositor's Greek Testament*, Vol. IV (William B. Eerdman's Publishing Co., Grand Rapids, MI, reprinted 1983), p. 118

6. Eph. 4:15

7. Harold Hoehner, *Ephesians – An Exegetical Commentary* (Baker Academic Books, Grand Rapids, MI, 2002), pp. 564-565

8. Marvin Vincent, *Word Studies in the New Testament*, Vol. III (William B. Eerdmans Publishing Co., Grand Rapids, MI, 1887, 1946), p. 392

9. Eph. 4:15 The Amplified Bible

10. Eph. 4:14 NAS

11. II Thes. 2:10-11

12. Dan. 9:13

13. Jn. 14:6

14. Jn. 1:14

15. I Jn. 1:1

16. I Jn. 1:1 Revised English Bible

17. Matt. 28:19-20

18. II Tim. 1:14; 2:2

19. James 3:1

20. Rom. 12:6-7

21. Acts 5:42

22. Acts 2:42 New English Bible

23. Clay Sterrett, *The Teacher and His Teaching* (can be ordered from CFC Literature, address in front of this book)

24. I Tim. 1:3-7

25. II Tim. 4:3

26. II Kings 7:9 New Living Translation

27. I Tim. 2:3-4

28. Luke 19:10

29. Luke 15:6

30. Donald McGavarn, *Effective Evangelism: A Theological Mandate* (Presbyterian and Reformed Publishing Company, Phillipsburg, NJ, 1988), p. 9

31. Watchman Nee, *Gleanings in the Field of Boaz* (Christian Fellowship Publishers, NY, 19 87), p. 127

32. George Barna, website The Barna Group. See www.barna.org

33. T. Austin Sparks, letter dated March 1943. From unpublished collection of his writings entitled, *View From the Mount of Vision*, by Three Brothers, order from Jon Moreshead, 605 Weeping Willow Drive, St. Charles, MO 63303.

34. II Pet. 3:9

CHAPTER FIVE NOTES: SHARED LEADERSHIP

1. Dick Mills, *The Spirit-Filled Believer's Daily Devotional* (Harrison House, Tulsa, OK, 1990), Nov. 2 devotional

2. Ex. 18:17-18

3. I Cor. 12:19 Phillips

4. Acts 20:17, 28

5. I Pet. 5:1-4

6. *The Classic Bible Commentary*, edited by Owen Collins (Crossway Books, Wheaton, IL, 1999), p. 465

7. Philip Schaff, *History of the Christian Church* (Eerdmans, Grand Rapids, MI, 1910), pp. 491-493.

8. Henry Thiessen, *Introductory Lectures in Systematic Theology* (Eerdmans, Grand Rapids, MI, 1949), p. 418

9. J. Rodman Williams, *Renewal Theology, Vol. 3* (Zondervan, Grand Rapids, MI, 1992), pp. 203, 219

10. Michael Green, *Evangelism Through the Local Church* (Thomas Nelson, Nashville, 1990), p. 102

11. Wayne Grudem, *Systematic Theology* (Zondervan, Grand Rapids, MI, 1994), pp. 912-913, 929

12. Eph. 4:11-12

13. George Barna, *The Power of Team Leadership* (WaterBrook Press, Colorado Springs, CO, 2001), p. 8

14. Op. cit., p .63

15. Op. cit., pp. 64-67. Barna also lists five other reasons.

16. In *The Diakonate*, Dale Rumble examines elders and the New Testament pattern for church leadership. (Order from Destiny Image, PO Box 310, Shippensburg, PA 17257)

17. Rom. 12:8 New English Bible

18. Isaiah 45:22 NJKV

19. Eph. 2:22

20. James Garrett, *New Testament Church Leadership*, (Doulos Press, PO Box 50130, Tulsa, OK 74150), pp. 231-239

21. Ex. 18:18

22. Barna, op. cit., p. 71

23. I Cor. 12:17

CHAPTER SIX NOTES: DESIRING MORE GOOD MEN FOR ELDERS

1. Tit. 1:5

2. I Tim. 5:22 New Living Translation

3. Acts 14:23 NAS

4. I Tim. 3:1-5. See a similar list in Tit. 1:6-9.

5. My two favorite chapters on this subject are found in *Biblical Eldership* by Alexander Strauch (Lewis and Roth Publishers), Chapter Four; and *New Testament Church Leadership*, by James Garrett (Doulos Press), Chapter Seven. Both books are available from us at CFC Literature.

6. I Thes. 5:12 KJV

7. There is a biblical precedent for "voting" on deacons (Acts 6:1-7). This was no popularity contest, however, but recognizing men who obviously had godly character.

8. Acts 20:28 Greek says the Holy Spirit *places* or *sets* the overseers in.

9. I Tim. 3:2 NAS

10. Psa. 68:11 NAS

11. Arthur Wallis, *China Miracle* (Kingsway Publications, Eastbourne, E. Sussex, G. Britian, 1985), pp. 88, 102

12. Phil. 4:3 Living Bible

13. Rom. 16:1-2. In Romans 16 Paul personally addresses 26 believers, most of whom were leaders and laborers in the church at Rome. Of these 26, eight are women who served faithfully in the local church. There is no greater commendation in the Scripture than that of a servant. Phoebe, in particular, is mentioned as a *deaconess* (marginal reading) or *servant*.

14. Acts 21:8-9

15. II Kings 4:8-10

16. Acts 12:12

17. Col. 4:15; Rom. 16:3-5

18. Acts 18:24-26. This couple is mentioned several times in Scripture, and it is notable that the wife, Priscilla, is always mentioned first. This couple hosted a church in their home and together had a teaching ministry. Priscilla may have been more of an initiator than her husband, and may have done more talking, but her ministry was under the authority of her husband. I have known of a few marriages in which the wife seems to be more the spiritual leader, yet functions effectively with the support of her believing husband.

19. Prov. 1:8; 6:20. Timothy's godly grandmother, Lois, is mentioned in Scripture, and during her life she may have never seen the fruit of her labor or realized the influence her grandson would have. She also had no idea that her name would forever be recorded in the pages of Scripture. The *sincere faith* which dwelt in Lois was passed on to Timothy's mother, Eunice, and also dwelt in Timothy (II Tim. 1:5). Through these two godly women, Timothy knew the holy Scriptures from infancy (II Tim. 3:15).

20. Tit. 2:3-5

21. I Tim. 2:11-12

22. Kenneth Wuest, *The New Testament: An Expanded Translation* (Eerdmans, Grand Rapids, MI, 1961)

23. I Cor. 14:34

24. I Cor. 14:35

25. I Cor. 11:5; 14:1-5,31 (notice "all"), 39. Also see Acts 21:8-9

26. Joseph Thayer, *Thayer's Greek-English Lexicon of the New Testament* (Associated Publishers, Grand Rapids, MI), p. 84

27. Jay Green, *Pocket Interlinear New Testament* (Baker Book House, Grand Rapids, MI, 1983)

28. II Tim. 1:5; 3:15

29. e.g., I Cor. 11:3; I Tim. 2:13-14

30. Eph. 2:22

31. The woman should pray for at least two male leaders to emerge. If it is only one man, there can be moral temptation with only one man and one woman working closely together. We must not be ignorant of this great temptation.

32. A good example of this is Apollos, who was earnest but not accurate in what he was teaching. Priscilla and Aquila took him into their home and taught him the word of God more thoroughly (Acts 18:24-26). As a result, Apollos became one of the great leaders in the early church.

CHAPTER SEVEN NOTES: MYTHS OF THE MINISTRY

1. *Shorter Oxford English Dictionary* (Oxford University Press, NY, 1973), p. 1876

2. II Cor. 3:5-6

3. Eph. 4:12 Amplified Bible, emphasis mine.

4. Matt. 20:26, 28

5. Gerhard Kittle, *Theological Dictionary of the New Testament, Vol. 2* (Eerdmans Publishing Co., Grand Rapids, MI, 1964), p. 84

6. *Webster's New Universal Unabridged Dictionary* (Barnes and Noble Books, NY, 1996)

7. I Pet. 2:9; Rev. 1:6

8. R. Paul Stevens, *Liberating the Laity* (Intervarsity Press, Downers Grove, IL, 1985), p. 23

9. I Cor. 14:26

10. I Cor. 14:40

11. Rom. 15:14 in Charles B. Williams, *The New Testament in the Language of the People* (Moody Press, Chicago, 1937)

12. William Barclay, *The Letters to the Corinthians, Revised Edition* (The Westminister Press, Philadelphia, 1975), p. 134

13. Eph. 5:33

14. Matt. 23:8

15. Alexander Strauch, *Biblical Eldership* (Lewis and Roth Publishers, Littleton, Co, 1986), pp. 98-99

16. Larry Peabody, *Secular Work is Full-time Service* (Christian Literature Crusade, Ft. Washington, PA, 1974), pp. 17-18

17. Lk. 16:10-11; Matt. 25:21

18. I Kings 19:19

19. Judges 6:11

20. Ex. 3:1

21. I Sam. 16:11

22. This account told in Stevens, *Liberating the Laity*.

23. Peabody, op. cit., pp. 37, 45

24. Derek Prince, *God is a Matchmaker* (Chosen Books, Old Tappan, NJ, 1986), p. 91

25. II Sam. 5:4

26. Gen. 41:46

27. Num. 4:3

28. Three good examples of younger men whom God used are: (1) Charles Spurgeon, who began working as a pastor at age 17 and was overseeing a large Baptist church in London at age 20. (2) Robert Murray McCheyne was a pastor who had a deeply spiritual influence in Scotland during his twenties but died a premature death at age 30. (3) David Brainerd, had a tremendous mission to North American Indians in the early 18th century, but after an illness, died at the young age of 29.

29. Judson Cornwall, *Leaders, Eat What You Serve* (Destiny Image, Shippensburg, PA, 1988), p. 52

30. I Cor. 9:7-14; I Tim. 5:17-18

31. e.g., Phil. 4:16

32. I Cor. 9:15 New English Bible

33. Acts 20:33-34

34. II Thes. 3:7-9

35. Strauch, op. cit., pp.76-77

36. Roland Allen, *The Compulsion of the Spirit* (Eerdmans Publishing Co., Grand Rapids, MI, 1983), p. 105

37. Charles Jefferson, *The Minister as Shepherd* (Christian Literature Crusade, Ft. Washington, PA, 1973), p. 79

38. Donald McGavran, *Effective Evangelism* (Presbyterian and Reformed Publishing Co., Phillipsburg, NJ, 1988), pp. 132-133

39. Ibid., p.132

CHAPTER EIGHT NOTES: GOD'S TRAINING PROGRAM FOR HIS SERVANTS

1. Acts 17:28

2. Andrew Bonar, *Memoir and Remains of R. M. M'Cheyne* (Banner of Truth Trust, Carlisle, PA, first printed in 1844; reprinted 1966), p. 28

3. Ibid., p. 31

4. Acts 7:22

5. G. M. Cowan, *Your Training or You* (InterVarsity Press, Downers Grove, IL)

6. DeVern Fromke, No Other Foundation (Sure Foundation, Indianapolis, IN, 1965), p. 136

7. Acts 9:20-24

8. II Cor. 11:23-33, esp. vs. 23, 32-33

9. II Cor. 6:3-4 NKJV

10. Report by Don Dunkerley, Dec. 1997 (Church Planting International, a missions agency in Pensacola, FL)

11. Here are ten recommended books:
    Abide in Christ, by Andrew Murray
    The Normal Christian Life, by Watchman Nee
    The Pursuit of God, by A. W. Tozer
    Ultimate Intention, by DeVem Fromke
    The Christian's Secret to a Happy Life, by Hannah Whitall Smith
    Calvary Road, by Roy Hession
    My Utmost for His Highest, by Oswald Chambers
    Power through Prayer, by E.M. Bounds
    Mere Christianity, by C. S. Lewis
    Spiritual Leadership, by J. Oswald Sanders

12. Eph. 4:11-12

13. Stevens, op. cit., p. 46

14. Alexander Hay, *The New Testament Order for Church and Missionary* (Published by the New Testament Missionary Union, Argentina, 1947), p. 488

15. T. A. Sparks, *Words of Wisdom and Revelation* (available from Three Brothers c/o Jon Moreshead, 605 Weeping Willow Drive, St. Charles, MO 63303), p. 34

16. Acts 14:23; Tit. 1:5 These elders were not transferred in; they were chosen from faithful local members.

17. Mk. 3:14-15

18. Matt. 10:1-11:1; Mk. 6:7-13; Lk. 9:1-6

19. Robert Coleman, *Master Plan of Evangelism* (Fleming Revell, Westwood, NJ, 1963), p. 38

20. Lk. 6:40 NAS

21. II Tim. 2:2 NAS

22. Acts 13:13; 20:4, 34

23. Gal. 1:18

24. Bauer, Arndt, and Gingrich, *A Greek-English Lexicon of the New Testament* (The University of Chicago Press, Chicago, 1957)

25. II Tim. 3:10-11 Phillips

26. Ralph Winter, *Faith and Renewal* magazine (Ann Arbor, MI), Nov. 1991 issue.

CHAPTER NINE NOTES: THE CHURCH IN THE HOME

1. II Cor. 6:16

2. Howard Snyder, *The Problem of Wineskins* (Inter-Varsity Press, Downers Grove, IL, 1975), p. 69

3. I Cor. 1:9

4. Acts 2:42 New English Bible

5. I John 1:3 New English Bible

6. Dietrich Bonhoeffer, *Life Together* (Harper and Row Publishers, NY, 1954)

7. Jerry Bridges, *True Fellowship* (NavPress, Colorado Springs, CO, 1985), p. 15

8. Mike Peters, *Meetings in His Kingdom* (Kingdom Publishing, P.O. Box 68309, Indianapolis, IN 46268, 1990), p. 79

9. Ps. 46:10

10. Haggai 1:9

11. Wayne Jacobsen, *A Passion for God's Presence* (Harvest House Publishers, Eugene, Oregon, 1987), p. 73

12. Matt. 18:20

13. e.g., Rom. 12:13; I Pet. 4:9: Tit. 1:8; Heb. 13:2

14. The Greek word for hospitality (*philoxenos*) literally means "a love for strangers."

15. Lk. 14:12-14

16. I Pet. 4:8

17. I Pet. 4:9

18. I Pet. 4:9 Phillips

19. Acts 2:46

20. Michael Green, *Evangelism in the Early Church* (Eerdman's Publishing Co., Grand Rapids, MI 1970), p. 236

21. Robert and Julia Banks, *The Home Church* (Albatross Books, Sutherland, Australia, 1986), p. 64

CHAPTER TEN NOTES: THE ROLE OF THE HOLY SPIRIT IN CORPORATE MEETINGS

1. II Cor. 13:14; Phil. 2:1

2. See Jn. 14:26. It is the Holy Spirit who *will lead us into all the truth.* Anytime we approach Scripture, it should not be as any other book. We should come humbly and ask the Holy Spirit to teach us, personally, his truth for this day. Apart from the Holy Spirit, the Bible will not be understood (I Cor. 2:14). Two good prayers to address to the Holy Spirit as we read the word of God are Ps. 119:18 and Eph. 1:17.

3. T. Austin-Sparks, *Words of Wisdom and Revelation* (Three Brothers, c/o Jon Moreshead, 605 Weeping Willow Drive, St. Charles, MO 63303), p. 37 Extra words added for clarity.

4. J. I. Packer, *Keep in Step With the Spirit* (Fleming Revell, Old Tappan, NJ, 1984), p. 9

5. Jean Walker, *Fool and Fanatic* (World Evangelization Crusade, 1980), p. 120

6. Rom. 8:14

7. Acts 7:51

8. Eph. 4:30

9. Heb. 10:29

10. I Thes. 5:19 NAS

11. I Thes. 5:19 Phillips

12. Gal. 3:3

13. Zech. 4:6

14. D.M. Lloyd-Jones, *Knowing the Times* (Banner of Truth Trust, Carlisle, PA, 1989), p. 30

15. Harry Verploegh, *A.W. Tozer – An Anthology* (Christian Publications, Camp Hill, PA, 1984), p. 114

16. Robert Girard, *Brethren, Hang Loose!* (Zondervan, Grand Rapids, MI, 1972), p. 73

17. e.g., I Cor. 11:2,23 NAS; 15:3; II Thes. 3:6,15 NAS

18. Jaroslav Pelikan as cited by Robert N. Bellah, *Habits of the Heart* (Harper and Row, NY, 1985), p. 140

19. Jer. 48:11 New Century Version

20. J.I. Packer, "The Comfort of Conservatism," article in *Power Religion*, ed. Michael Horton (Moody Press, Chicago, 1992), p. 289

21. Matt. 15:6

22. Matt. 15:6 *The New Testament in the Language of the People* by Charles Williams (Moody Press, Chicago, 1937)

23. Lk. 10:27

24. Prov. 16:9 Living Bible

25. Michael Green, *Evangelism Through the Local Church* (Thomas Nelson Pub., Nashville, TN, 1990), p. 105

26. I Cor. 14:26

27. I Cor. 14:33,40

28. I Cor. 14:30-31 Phillips

29. Harry Verploegh, *Oswald Chambers: The Best From All His Books* (Thomas Nelson, Nashville, TN, 1987), p. 273

30. Col. 3:3

31. I Cor. 12:28 Today's English Version

32. I Cor. 12:28 Revised English Bible

33. Gerhard Kittle, *Theological Dictionary of the New Testament, Vol. 3* (Eerdmans, Grand Rapids, MI, 1965), p. 1036

34. I Cor. 14:26 The Message

35. William Barclay, *The Letters to the Corinthians, Revised Edition* (The Westminister Press, Philadelphia, 1975), pp. 134-135

CHAPTER ELEVEN NOTES: PROPERLY ASSESSING MINISTRIES IN THE CHURCH

1. Eph. 4:11-13

2. For starters, I recommend the following books. On apostles, I suggest Jim Garrett, *New Testament Church Leadership* (Available through Doulos Press, PO Box 50130, Tulsa, OK 74150-0130 or go to the website: jim@doulospress.org for some free download articles. An excellent article, written in 2005, is "Translocal Ministry in the New Testament Church," which covers apostles,

prophets, and evangelists.) For prophets, I recommend Wayne Grudem, *The Gift of Prophecy* (Crossway Books, Wheaton, Il, 1988, 2000) and Graham Cooke, *Developing Your Prophetic Gifting* (Chosen Books, Grand Rapids, MI, 1994, 2003)For evangelists, I like Roger Carswell, *And Some Evangelists* (Christian Focus Publications, Geanies House, Fearn, Ross-shire, IV20, ITW, Great Britian. This book may be available through Christian Book Distributors or check the website at www.christianfocus.com) and Michael Green, *Evangelism Through the Local Church* (Thomas Nelson Publishers, Nashville, 1992)

3. Acts 20:28-31

4. Jn. 10:7-13

5. Acts 14:26-28

6. Rev. 2:2

7. I Cor. 14:29, 37-38 NAS

8. II Tim. 4:3-4

9. II Cor. 1:24 NRSV emphasis mine

10. W.E. Vine, *Vine's Expository Dictionary of Old and New Testament Words* (Fleming Revell Co., Old Tappan, NJ, 1981), p. 280

11. See I Cor. 13:7 which says *love believes all things* (NAS). Moffatt's translation says, *Love is . . . always slow to expose, always eager to believe the best, always hopeful.*

12. Prov. 14:15 New English Bible

13. I Thes. 5:21

14. I Thes 5:12 KJV

15. Ps. 105:15

16. I Sam. 16:6, 13; II Sam. 19:21

17. I Sam. 20

18. II Sam. 12

19. II Sam. 16:5-10 Living Bible

20. Quote from Edwin and Lillian Harvey, *To Judge or Not to Judge* (Harvey & Tait, Hampton, TN, 1986), p. 32

21. II Pet. 2:15

22. Watchman Nee, *Rethinking the Work*, published under the title, *The Church and the Work II*, by Christian Fellowship Publishers, Richmond, VA, 1982), p. 46

23. I Pet. 5:2

24. Lk. 12:15

25. D. Martyn Lloyd-Jones, *Studies in the Sermon on the Mount, Vol. 2* (Eerdmans Publishing Co., Grand Rapids, MI, 1960), p. 94

26. I Jn. 4:1

27. I Tim. 4:1

28. I Cor. 12:10

29. For example, prophecy may be caused by the Holy Spirit (I Cor. 12:8-10), the human spirit (Ezek. 13:2), or a demonic spirit (Matt. 24:11, 24; Acts 16:16-18).

30. Jonathan Edwards, *The Works of Jonathan Edwards, Vol. 2* (Banner of Truth, Edinburgh,1974), pp. 266-269

31. A.W. Tozer, *The Best of A.W. Tozer* (Christian Publications, Camp Hill, PA, 1987), p. 190

32. Acts 20:28

33. Eph. 4:13

CHAPTER TWELVE NOTES: PRACTICAL OUTWORKINGS OF CHURCH UNITY

1. Rom. 15:5-7

2. Albert Barnes, *Barnes' Notes on the New Testament* (Kregel Publications, Grand Rapids, MI, 1962), p. 911

3. Acts 7:23-26; Rom. 9:3

4 John 1:40-41; 7:3

5. I Pet. 1:3,17, 22-23; Heb. 2:9-11

6. I Pet. 2:17

7. Eph. 3:10

8. Henry Thayer, *Thayer's Greek-English Lexicon of the New Testament* (Associated Publishers, Grand Rapids, MI), p. 529. Greek word *polupoikilos*

9. Gen. 37:3 Septuagint, Greek word *poikilos*

10. Eph. 3:10 Revised English Bible

11. Gerald Sittser, *Loving Across our Differences* (Intervarsity Press, Downers Grove, IL, 1994), p. 246

12. Rom. 14:4 Phillips

13. Gal. 2:8 NIV

14. II Cor. 10:13-15

15. Lk. 9:49-50

16. Derek Prince, *Pastoral Renewal Magazine* (Ann Arbor, MI)

17. *World Book Encyclopedia*, article on "Muscle," (Field Enterprises, Chicago, 1977)

18. Prince, op. cit.

19. Rom. 14:1, 13, 21; 15:5

20. Robert C. Chapman, *Choice Sayings* (Gospel Tract Publications, Glasgow, 1988), p. 86

21. Matthew Henry's comment on I Peter 5. From 3000 *Quotations from the Writings of Matthew Henry*, William Summers, Compiler (Fleming Revell Co., Grand Rapids, MI, 1982), p. 138

22. Prov. 13:10 NKJV

23. Graham Miller, *Calvin's Wisdom* (The Banner of Truth Trust, Carlisle, PA, 1992), pp.153-155

24. Jonathan Edwards, *Thoughts on the Revival*, quoted in Richard Lovelace, *Dynamics of Spiritual Life* (InterVarsity Press, Downers Grove, IL, 1979), pp. 245-246

25. I Cor. 12:21

26. Edwards, op. cit., p. 247

27. Phil. 2:3-4

28. Leslie Flynn, *Great Church Fights* (Victor Books, Wheaton, IL, 1976), p. 91

29. C. S. Lewis, *The Joyful Christian* (MacMillan Publishing Co., NY, 1977), p. 141

30. Col. 3:13

31. Arndt and Gingrich, *A Greek-English Lexicon of the New Testament* (University of Chicago Press, 1957), pp. 125-126; and Thayer's Greek-English Lexicon (Associated Publishers)

32. I Pet. 2:23

33. Lk. 6:27-28

34. I Cor. 13:5

35. Matt. 18:35; also see Lk. 17:3-10 where it indicates forgiveness is simply "our duty."

36. Amy Carmichael, *If* (Christian Literature Crusade, Ft. Washington, PA), p.48

37. *Webster's Seventh New Collegiate Dictionary* (G. & C. Merriam Company, Springfield, MA, 1971)

38. Jer. 31:34. Also see Is. 43:25

39. Jay Adams, *from Forgiven to Forgiving* (Victor Books, Wheaton, IL, 1989), p. 86

40. Gen. 41:51-52

41. Gen. 40:15

42. William MacDonald, *Believer's Bible Commentary: New Testament* (Thomas Nelson Publishers, Nashville 1990), p. 1073

43. Eph. 4:2-3 NAS

44. Same Greek word is also used in Mk. 9:19

45. Eph. 4:2 The Amplified Bible

46. Robert Peterson and Alexander Strauch, *Agape Leadership* (Lewis and Roth Publishers, Littleton, Co, 1991). p. 32

47. Gerald L. Sittser, *Loving Across Our Differences* (InterVarsity Press, Downers Grove, IL, 1994), p. 64

48. The author has written a couple chapters on this subject: "Judgment in the Church" in *The Judgments of God*. Available from the same address as this book.

49. Charles Spurgeon, *John Ploughman's Talks* (Whitaker House, Springdale, PA, 1993) pp. 69-71

CHAPTER THIRTEEN NOTES: THE LOVE OF GOD – THE PERFECT BOND OF UNITY

1. Col. 3:14 NAS

2. Andrew Murray, *The Believer's Secret of Living Like Christ* (Bethany House Publishers, Minneapolis, MN, 1985), p. 80

3. Paul Billheimer, *Love Covers* (Christian Literature Crusade, Ft. Washington, PA, 1981), p. 88, 29

4. I Cor. 13:5 The Amplified Bible

5. Juan Carlos Ortiz, *God is Closer than You Think* (Servant Publications, Ann Arbor, MI, 1992), pp. 172-173

6. John Pollock, *George Whitefield and the Great Awakening* (Lion Publishing, Belleville, MI, 1972), p. 190

7. Eph. 4:16

8. I Cor. 13:1-3

9. John 13:34

10. I have written a chapter on the subject of meekness in *Spiritual Precautions* (available from the same address as this book). Some of this information is adapted from this chapter.

11. Gerhard Friedrich, *Theological Dictionary of the New Testament*, Vol. 6 (Eerdmans, Grand Rapids, MI, 1968), p. 645

12. Ibid., p. 645

13. II Tim. 2:24-25 Living Bible

14. I Cor. 13:5 RSV and Rom. 12:10

15. Genesis 13

16. Francis Schaeffer, "The Mark of the Christian," from *The Great Evangelical Disaster* (Crossway Books, Westchester, IL), p. 182

17. John Pollock, *George Whitefield and the Great Awakening* (Lion Publishing Co., Belleville, MI, 1972), p. 185

18. Ibid., p. 242

19. Ibid., p. 245

20. Stephen Clark, article in *Pastoral Renewal* (Ann Arbor, MI) April 1987 issue.

21. Whitney J. Dough, compiler, *Sayings of E. Stanley Jones* (Providence House Publishers, Franklin, TN, 1994), p. 136

22. Col. 3:14 NKJV

23. Eph. 3:16-19

24. Francis Schaeffer, op. cit., p. 182

25. John Pollock, *Moody*, (Zondervan, Grand Rapids, MI, 1963), p. 198

26. Charles Colson, *Who Speaks for God*, (Crossway Books, Westchester, IL, 1985), p. 53

CHAPTER FOURTEEN NOTES: THE CHURCH IN THE CITY

1. I Cor. 1:2

2. e.g., I Cor. 1:11-12

3. Acts 9:31 NAS

4. Gal. 1:2

5. I Cor. 16:19

6. J. N. Darby, *Collected Works of J.N. Darby*, Ecclesiastical Vol. 1, edited by William Kelly (Believers Bookshelf, Sunbury, PA)

7. Matt. 5:14

8. Matt. 5:14-16

9. Mark 13:1

10. Eph. 2:21

11. Rev. 1:20

12. Ex. 37:17-24

13. I Cor. 12:20

14. Roland Allen, *Missionary Methods: St. Paul's or Ours?*, (Eerdmans Pub. Co., Grand Rapids, MI, 1962), p. 128

15. W. M. Douglas, *Andrew Murray and His Message* (Baker Book House, Grand Rapids, MI, 1981), p. 136

16. Ibid., p. 136

17. I Cor. 3:21-22

18. Rom. 12:5 The Amplified Bible

19. I Cor. 12:22-23 Living Bible

20. Eph. 4:13 [emphasis mine]

21. Ps. 133

22. Frank Damazio, *The Making of a Leader* (Church Life Library, Eugene, OR, 1987), p. iii

23. Richard Baxter, *The Reformed Pastor* (The Banner of Truth Trust, Edinburgh, 1656, 1829), p. 47

24. II Chron. 30:1, 11-13

25. II Chron. 30:21-23

26. Col. 4:15-16

27. I Thes. 2:14

28. I Cor. 16:1-4

29. Peter Wagner, *The Rising Revival* (Renew Books, Ventura, CA, 1998), pp. 186-187

30. Ibid., pp. 187-188

31. Phil. 1:27

32. Lk. 5:5-7

33. Neh. 2

34. Jdg. 20:1, 11

35. Zeph. 3:9

CHAPTER FIFTEEN NOTES: GOD'S GLORIOUS CHURCH –THE BRIDE OF CHRIST

1. Eph. 5:25-27

2. Song of Songs 3:11

3. Paul Billheimer, *Destined for the Throne* (Christian Literature Crusade, Ft. Washington, PA, 1975), p. 25

4. Rom. 8:19 Phillips

5. I John 3:2

6. I Cor. 15:51-52

7. Heb. 12:1

8. Heb. 12:22-24

9. Deut. 18:11; Lev. 19:31

10. I Cor. 1:4-5

11. *Westminster Confession of Faith* (25.5), 1643-46.

12. Lance Lambert, from spoken message "Weapons of our Warfare," July 1, 1993, from Christian Tape Ministry, Richmond, VA.

13. Eph. 2:10

14. Eph. 2:22

15. Col. 2:10 NAS

16. I Cor. 1:30; II Cor. 5:21

17. II Pet. 1:3

18. Ps. 87:3, 7

19. Ps. 50:2 NAS

20. Rev. 1:12; 2:1

21. Watchman Nee, *What Shall This Man Do?* (Christian Literature Crusade, Ft. Washington, PA, 1961), pp.161-166

22. Matt. 16:18

23. Ralph M. Smith, "Upon This Rock," in *Spirit of Revival* magazine, April 1994 issue (Life Action Ministries, Buchanan, MI)